I0100021

The Inner Work of Relationships:

Building Better Relationships Through Self-Discovery and Compassion

PUBLISHED BY Ember Maple Editions

Table of contents

Introduction: The Mirror of Connection

"We do not see things as they are, we see them as we are." – Anaïs Nin

There's a moment in nearly every human life when we pause—sometimes after heartbreak, sometimes in the middle of conflict, sometimes while lying next to someone we love—and ask: *Why do my relationships feel so hard? Why do I keep ending up in the same patterns, even when the people change?*

It's tempting to look outward for answers. We blame bad timing, misaligned values, toxic behaviors, or simply "the wrong person." These explanations bring temporary relief. They externalize our pain, giving us someone or something to hold responsible. But they rarely bring lasting change. Because beneath every disappointment in connection, there's a mirror—one we rarely dare to look into. That mirror is ourselves.

This book begins with an invitation: to turn inward. Not because you are the problem, but because you are the portal. You are the one constant in every relationship you've ever had. And within you lies the map—not just to understanding what went wrong, but to creating what could go beautifully right.

This is not another guide that teaches you how to communicate better, how to set firmer boundaries, or how to "manifest" your ideal partner. Those tools matter, and they have their place. But tools alone don't change your wiring. They don't reach the parts of you that quietly sabotage connection, that repeat old wounds in new packaging, that long to be loved but don't always know how to let love in.

Real transformation in relationships begins with something deeper than technique. It begins with self-honesty. With the

5

courage to sit in your own discomfort and ask, *What am I bringing into this relationship—consciously or unconsciously? What beliefs, expectations, fears, or unresolved pain live inside me, shaping how I relate to others?*

When we start to ask these questions, the world shifts. The people around us don't suddenly become perfect. Circumstances don't magically align. But our perception evolves. And because perception is the filter through which we experience reality, everything changes.

We've all heard some version of the idea that "relationships are mirrors." But few truly grasp its radical implications. Every judgment we make of others—he's too cold, she's too needy, they're too controlling—points to something inside us. It might reflect a disowned part of ourselves, a wound we haven't healed, or a standard we secretly hold ourselves to. That doesn't mean we excuse harmful behavior or abandon healthy boundaries. But it does mean we stop pretending that "they" are the only ones who need fixing.

Imagine walking through a house of mirrors, where each person you encounter shows you a different angle of your inner world. Some mirrors flatter you; others distort you painfully. Some reflect old memories, ancestral patterns, or cultural scripts. Some show you who you wish you were; others confront you with who you fear you might be. And some—those rare and precious ones—reveal your essence beneath all the layers. Relationships, when viewed this way, become not just emotional experiences, but spiritual teachers.

This is not a new idea. Mystics, poets, and psychologists across centuries have echoed this truth in different languages. Rumi wrote, "The wound is the place where the Light enters you." Carl Jung spoke of the "shadow"—the parts of ourselves we deny and project onto others. Contemporary neuroscience confirms that our early attachment patterns shape how we see and interact with the world. And modern trauma research shows us how unhealed pain can distort both perception and behavior. The mirror is not just metaphor—it is mechanism.

To understand this, we need to look not only at who we are today, but at how we got here. As children, we learn about love through experience, not definition. If love was inconsistent, we may come to equate it with anxiety. If connection was conditional, we might believe we must perform to be worthy. If we were never truly seen, we may struggle to see others. These early templates don't disappear with age. They get buried, disguised, and reenacted.

Adult relationships are the stage upon which our earliest dramas get replayed. But they also offer us the chance to rewrite the script. Each time we're triggered, each time we feel rejected, unseen, or overwhelmed, we're being offered a mirror: not just of the other person's behavior, but of our own wounds and narratives. It's not always comfortable. In fact, it rarely is. But it's the doorway to liberation.

Because once we see the pattern, we can choose. We can stop blaming and start healing. We can become conscious of our defaults, our reactions, our fears. And in that awareness, we regain agency. We no longer unconsciously seek partners who confirm our deepest fears. We no longer parent our partners or project our unmet needs onto them. We stop demanding that others fill holes we haven't tended to ourselves.

This doesn't mean relationships become easy. But they become more real. Less about performance, more about presence. Less about perfection, more about truth. And in that shift, something beautiful happens: intimacy deepens. Because nothing is more attractive, more magnetic, more trustworthy than someone who knows themselves.

Self-awareness is not self-obsession. It's not naval-gazing or perpetual self-analysis. It's a form of humility. It says: "I don't know everything about myself. But I'm willing to look. I'm willing to question my assumptions, revisit my wounds, and take responsibility for what I bring into this world." That willingness is rare. But it is the foundation of mature love.

So what does it mean, practically, to "do the inner work"? It means becoming curious instead of reactive. It means noticing your patterns, not just in thought, but in your nervous system— in how your body tenses, how your breath changes, how your voice shifts. It means tracking the stories you tell yourself when someone doesn't text back or when your partner withdraws. It means sitting with your discomfort without immediately needing to fix or flee it.

It also means compassion. Because once you start looking inward, you'll discover things you don't like. You'll find pettiness, insecurity, jealousy, defensiveness, control. You'll find wounds you thought you'd healed, needs you thought you'd outgrown. And your task is not to judge those parts, but to meet them. To understand why they exist. To hold them with kindness, without letting them run the show.

Inner work is also relational work. It doesn't happen in a vacuum. We need others to trigger us, to awaken our blind spots, to stretch us into growth. That's why the mirror metaphor is so powerful: we can't see ourselves clearly without reflection. But when we approach our relationships with this awareness, even conflict becomes sacred. Even rupture becomes opportunity.

And here's the paradox: the more you understand yourself, the less you need others to be different. That doesn't mean you accept mistreatment. It means you stop trying to extract validation from people who can't give it. You stop chasing love through performance or withdrawal. You start relating from wholeness, not from lack.

In this space, boundaries become acts of love, not punishment. Communication becomes a bridge, not a battleground. Vulnerability becomes strength, not exposure. And connection becomes a dance of two whole beings choosing each other—not out of need, but out of truth.

This is the heart of the journey we are about to take. Over the pages that follow, we will explore the anatomy of the mirror. We'll examine how childhood experiences shape adult patterns, how trauma impacts our ability to connect, how the nervous system influences relationship dynamics. We'll dive into attachment styles, emotional regulation, projection, reparenting, forgiveness, and spiritual alignment. But we'll do so not as passive observers, but as active participants—each page inviting you not just to learn, but to look.

Because if there's one truth that changes everything, it's this: your relationships are not problems to be solved. They are mirrors to be understood. And once you begin to understand, the entire landscape of your life begins to shift—from confusion to clarity, from conflict to connection, from seeking love to becoming it.

You are not here to be perfect. You are here to be aware. To grow. To love, not blindly, but wisely. And to let every relationship—past, present, and future—become a mirror through which you meet not only others, but your truest self.

Chapter 1: The Archaeology of Self – Excavating Your Relational Patterns

"Until you make the unconscious conscious, it will direct your life and you will call it fate." — Carl Jung

1.1 Mapping Your Emotional Blueprint

If your relationships feel like déjà vu—if you keep dating the same type of person, having the same fights, or ending up in the same emotional spiral—it's not coincidence. It's programming.

Not in the tech sense, but in the deeply human sense. Emotional programming happens when we're still too young to realize we're learning. The way your caregiver looked at you (or didn't), the tone of their voice, the way they handled your sadness, your joy, your anger—these became instructions for how love works. How safety feels. What to expect when you reach for closeness. And unless we bring these internal maps to light, we'll keep using them to navigate adulthood, unaware that we're being guided by outdated charts drawn by a child trying to survive.

This chapter is about pulling those blueprints out from the dark corners of your psyche. Not to blame or judge your past—but to reclaim your authorship in the present.

We begin with what most people ignore: your emotional themes. These are the undercurrents that shape how you feel in relationships, even when logic tells you otherwise. For example, you might tell yourself that your partner is just busy, but feel the same gut-level abandonment you felt as a child when your parent forgot to pick you up from school. Or maybe you've been told your whole life that you're "too sensitive," and now you silence your own needs to avoid being labeled dramatic. These feelings aren't irrational—they're echoes. And until you recognize their original source, you'll keep misinterpreting current situations through the lens of your earliest emotional wounds.

Start here: think of your last few relational breakdowns—not just romantic ones, but friendships, family, colleagues. What emotions came up repeatedly? Were you anxious, like you were walking on eggshells? Did you feel unseen, like you had to perform to be acknowledged? Did you retreat, convinced that nobody really understands you? These emotional signatures are clues. They're not random; they are deeply embedded messages from your past, surfacing to be heard.

What makes these themes so persistent is that they aren't just mental—they live in your nervous system. They fire before logic kicks in. That's why your heart races at a certain tone of voice, why you freeze when someone expresses anger, why a simple "we need to talk" sends your system into panic. Your body remembers what your conscious mind has long forgotten.

But this emotional blueprint didn't form in a vacuum. It's part of a much larger inheritance. Before you could speak, you were absorbing your environment—not just through experience, but through observation. You watched how your parents or caregivers related to each other. How conflict was handled—or avoided. How affection was expressed—or withheld. If love looked like criticism, you might have internalized that love must be earned. If peace came only through silence, you may have learned to equate harmony with self-erasure.

This is where we begin to trace the generational thread.

Because your emotional blueprint is not just yours—it's a chapter in a longer story. Look at your family with the eyes of a historian.

What themes do you see repeated? Was there a culture of silence around emotion? Did your caregivers grow up in survival mode, where emotions were luxuries they couldn't afford? Were vulnerability and tenderness mocked or shamed? These legacies don't disappear—they mutate. And you carry them, even if you've never named them.

Often, we resist looking back because we don't want to feel disloyal. "My parents did their best." Of course they did. This is not about blame—it's about understanding. Acknowledging the patterns you inherited doesn't dishonor your family; it liberates you. You can love someone deeply and still recognize how their unhealed wounds shaped your own.

And this brings us to the heart of relational archaeology: attachment.

Attachment is more than a theory—it's the foundation of how you experience intimacy. From the moment you're born, your nervous system is scanning: *Am I safe? Will someone respond when I cry? Will they be consistent? Can I relax into connection, or do I need to earn love to survive?*

These questions were answered long before you had language. And whatever answer you internalized became your attachment strategy. If love was steady and responsive, you likely developed secure attachment—you trust that connection is safe and available. But if love was unpredictable, you may have developed anxious attachment—hyper-vigilant to cues of rejection, needing constant reassurance. If love was neglectful or overwhelming, you may lean avoidant—believing it's safer to stay distant and self-sufficient. And for some, where love and danger were intertwined, disorganized attachment emerges—a push-pull dynamic where closeness and fear coexist.

These strategies aren't flaws. They were solutions. Brilliant, adaptive responses to your specific environment. But as adults, they can become cages. An anxious person might cling to someone emotionally unavailable, trying to prove their worth. An avoidant person might back away the moment intimacy deepens, convinced they'll be engulfed. A disorganized person might ricochet between extremes, craving love but expecting betrayal.

And here's the twist: we often unconsciously choose partners who confirm our original story. Not because we enjoy suffering, but because the psyche seeks familiarity. We repeat the pattern, hoping to resolve it. Hoping this time, love will stay. This time, we'll be chosen. This time, we'll feel enough.

But healing doesn't come from reenactment. It comes from awareness.

When you start recognizing your emotional blueprint, your generational inheritance, your attachment strategy—you stop operating on autopilot. You create a gap between stimulus and response. You notice when you're reacting from an old wound. You ask yourself, *Is this about the present moment—or is this the past echoing through my body?*

It's in that space that change begins.

Let's be clear: awareness doesn't mean your nervous system suddenly relaxes. You'll still get triggered. You'll still have the urge to run, to chase, to shut down, to people-please. But now, you'll know why. You'll have context. You'll be able to pause and offer yourself what you needed back then—validation, comfort, safety. And when you do, you begin to rewire.

This work isn't linear. You don't "fix" your attachment style and then ride off into securely bonded bliss. It's a lifelong excavation. There will be layers. Resistance. Regression. But each layer you uncover gives you more freedom, more clarity, more capacity to love and be loved without the baggage of unconscious expectation.

It also shifts how you see others. Once you understand that people relate from their own emotional blueprints, you soften. You stop taking things so personally. You realize that someone's withdrawal may be their old strategy for safety, not a reflection of your worth. You stop trying to *change* people and start relating to them with curiosity, boundaries, and compassion.

You might also realize that some people can't meet you where you are—and that's okay. You don't need to fix them. You need to honor your growth.

Mapping your emotional blueprint doesn't mean digging forever into your past. It means gathering the essential information you need to break the loop. To name your patterns. To see your part— not in a way that blames you, but in a way that empowers you.

You're not doomed to repeat what you inherited. You are the living proof that patterns can end with you. That love can look different. That what you lacked, you can learn to give yourself— and then offer to others, not from depletion, but from overflow.

As we move forward, remember: this is not an intellectual exercise. It's embodied. Emotional. Sometimes painful. But it is also the most liberating work you can do. Because the moment you stop calling your patterns "fate," you reclaim your power to choose something new.

You're not broken. You're patterned. And every pattern can be rewritten—once it's seen. That's where we begin.

1.2 The Shadow Self in Relationships

There's a paradox at the heart of human connection: the very qualities we most deny in ourselves often become the qualities we're most sensitive to in others. The deeper you go into your inner landscape, the more you begin to notice this strange mirroring effect. A partner's arrogance might provoke rage not just because it's unpleasant, but because you've spent your whole life repressing your own assertiveness. A friend's emotional neediness might irritate you because you were taught to keep your own needs hidden. We often believe we're reacting to *them*—but we're actually confronting an exiled part of *us*. This is the realm of the shadow.

Carl Jung gave us the language of the "shadow self"—the unconscious repository of traits we disown, suppress, or shame. But the shadow isn't limited to what's "bad" or dangerous. It also includes the parts of us that were once vibrant and whole but got shut down to secure acceptance. Your playfulness, sensuality, ambition, creativity, anger—any part of you that wasn't welcomed as a child may now live in shadow. And because the psyche resists emptiness, those disowned aspects don't just disappear. They reappear—on the faces of others.

This is projection. Not in the casual sense of saying "you're projecting" during an argument, but in the deeper psychological mechanism by which we unconsciously relocate a disowned part of ourselves onto someone else. You might think your partner is controlling, never recognizing that you too fear losing control. You might accuse your friend of being emotionally unavailable, never seeing how you yourself have built walls around your heart. Projection distorts perception. It turns people into screens upon which we play the old films of our inner life.

What makes this process so difficult to catch is how real it feels. When you're in the grip of a projection, your nervous system reacts as if it's responding to a true external threat or flaw. You're convinced you're "just being honest" or that you're "seeing clearly," when in fact, you're wearing a lens crafted by your unresolved emotional history. To become aware of projection is to begin dismantling illusion—not in the mystical sense, but in the very practical sense of no longer mistaking your unhealed parts for someone else's faults.

And then there's the flip side: attraction.

So often, the people we fall for are not random. They are carriers of something we've buried in ourselves. You may find yourself irresistibly drawn to someone who's bold, reckless, and unapologetic—while you've spent your life being careful, measured, and responsible. On the surface, it might look like opposites attract. But underneath, your attraction is a signal from the soul. That person represents a lost piece of you.

This is what Jungians might call "shadow attraction." It's the gravitational pull we feel toward people who reflect back our unlived potential. They awaken something in us—not because they complete us, but because they embody the very traits we've disowned. These relationships often start with electricity. There's a sense of familiarity, of destiny. But over time, what once fascinated can begin to irritate or even enrage. The same person who felt intoxicatingly free now feels chaotic. The one who seemed confident now feels domineering. And we wonder: *What changed?*

What changed is that the unconscious contract has been revealed. You didn't just fall for them—you fell for what they symbolized. And the moment they stop serving that symbolic function, the relationship becomes confusing. But if you can see it, if you can name it, then the real work can begin. Instead of trying to possess that quality through another, you can integrate it within yourself.

You can explore where your own wildness, your own sensuality, your own ambition went—and invite it home.

Relationships, then, become alchemical. They expose your fragments not to break you, but to offer you wholeness. This is especially true when you're triggered.

To be triggered is to have a disproportionate emotional reaction to something someone said or did. A seemingly small comment sends you spiraling. Your partner's slight withdrawal activates panic. A friend's success makes you feel small. Most people try to suppress or rationalize these feelings. But in the lens of inner work, a trigger is sacred. It's a flare fired by the unconscious, signaling that something hidden is asking to be seen.

Triggers aren't signs that something's wrong. They're invitations. They show you where your shadow lives. If you can pause—really pause—when a trigger hits, and ask, *What does this remind me of? What emotion is underneath this? What story am I telling myself right now?*—then the trigger becomes a portal. It opens the door to buried memories, false beliefs, and emotional debris that have been quietly dictating your relational life.

This isn't about spiritual bypassing. We don't use the idea of triggers to avoid setting boundaries or to stay in unhealthy situations. It's not about staying in the fire longer than is safe. But it is about recognizing that the fire holds meaning. That the people who activate you most intensely are often the ones who carry keys to parts of you you've forgotten.

Every relationship, in this sense, becomes a mirror—but not just a mirror of who you are. A mirror of who you could become. And the more willing you are to look at your projections, your attractions, and your triggers with curiosity rather than blame, the more you grow. The more you stop searching for "the right person" and start becoming the person who no longer unconsciously recreates the past.

The shadow isn't an enemy. It's a reservoir of potential. A storehouse of everything you once were, and everything you could be again. And relationships, with all their messiness, are the crucible in which the shadow can be reclaimed—not through analysis alone, but through the raw, intimate, often painful experience of relating.

1.3 Somatic Awareness and Relational Intelligence

You may believe your relationships are being sabotaged by communication issues, personality differences, or bad luck. But often, what's really happening is that your nervous system is stuck in an old script. A script written not in words, but in sensations. Tight chest. Shallow breath. A knot in the stomach. An impulse to run, to lash out, to disappear. These aren't just feelings—they're data. And if you want to change how you relate, you need to start listening to your body.

Somatic awareness is the ability to sense what's happening in your physical body and interpret it as meaningful. Not in a mystical way, but in a neurobiological one. Your body is a memory vault. Long before you could talk, it was learning what connection felt like. Was it safe? Was it predictable? Did it hurt? Those early bodily experiences got encoded in your nervous system, creating templates that still play out every time you get close to someone.

If you grew up in a household where emotions were dangerous or dismissed, your body learned to constrict. If your safety was ever compromised—through neglect, chaos, or inconsistency—

your system adapted by becoming hypervigilant or numb. These adaptations aren't flaws. They're signs of intelligence. But they don't just fade with age. They become the unseen authors of your reactions.

In adult relationships, these stored patterns show up in moments you least expect. You find yourself freezing during an argument, unable to speak. Or you explode with emotion that feels out of proportion to what just happened. Or you shut down completely—not because you don't care, but because your body believes it's protecting you from harm. This is what trauma therapist Peter Levine describes as "the body keeping the score." Your body doesn't forget.

The key to change is awareness—not just cognitive, but somatic. You need to develop what we might call *relational intelligence*— the ability to read your own internal signals in real time, especially in the heat of connection. This means noticing when your breath shortens or your shoulders tighten. Recognizing the early signs of fight, flight, freeze, or fawn. And instead of overriding those signals, you slow down. You create space. You ask yourself, *What's happening in my body right now? What does it need?*

This might sound simple, but it's radical. Because most of us were taught to live from the neck up. We solve problems with logic. We prepare scripts for hard conversations. We analyze our partners or write them off as emotionally immature. But beneath all that analysis, our bodies are screaming for attention. And unless we include them in the process, transformation remains partial.

Somatic work also helps us recognize how our childhood survival strategies still operate today. If you learned to keep the peace at all costs, you might still fawn in relationships—over-giving, shape-shifting, anticipating needs. If you learned that conflict led to chaos, you might still avoid honest conversations, even when avoidance creates more damage. If love was unpredictable, you might cling tightly or withdraw entirely. These behaviors once kept you safe. But now, they limit intimacy. They make it hard to show up authentically, to stay when it's hard, or to trust when it's good.

And here's where it gets subtle: these patterns are often invisible to the mind, but obvious to the body. Your thoughts may say, "I'm fine," but your chest tells a different story. Your smile may look calm, but your jaw is clenched. Your words may sound open, but your shoulders are curled inward, protecting your heart. Learning to decode these signals isn't just self-awareness—it's self-liberation.

Another profound gift of somatic awareness is the development of energetic and emotional boundaries. Many people struggle with where they end and others begin. They absorb emotions like sponges, confuse others' needs with their own, or feel guilty for saying no. These aren't just psychological issues—they're somatic ones. Without a clear felt sense of your own body, it's nearly impossible to discern what's yours and what isn't.

Developing somatic boundaries means learning to feel your own inner space. To ground yourself in your body, even when someone else is dysregulated. To stay with your own breath, your own sensations, your own truth. This doesn't mean disconnecting from others. It means staying connected to yourself *while* staying present with them. That is relational maturity. That is nervous system sovereignty.

The beauty of this work is that it's always available. Your body is with you in every interaction. You don't need years of therapy to begin noticing your breath. You don't need perfect language to sense your feet on the floor. You simply need willingness.

Willingness to pause, to listen, to feel. And in that pause, you start to change the script.

Over time, as your somatic awareness deepens, your relationships begin to feel different. You become less reactive, more anchored. You stop abandoning yourself in moments of tension. You become someone who can stay—with yourself, with your partner, with discomfort. And from that grounded place, love becomes less about strategy and more about truth.

This is the foundation of all relational healing. Not just insight, but integration. Not just theory, but embodiment. When your body becomes a safe place to inhabit, relationships stop being battlegrounds. They become places of co-regulation, growth, and deep presence. And that, perhaps, is the most intimate gift of all.

Chapter 2: The Compassion Revolution – Transforming Self-Criticism into Self-Acceptance

"You, yourself, as much as anybody in the entire universe, deserve your love and affection." — Buddha

In the modern mythology of self-improvement, there's an insidious character lurking in the background. It wears many faces—discipline, ambition, humility—but its true name is self-criticism. It's the inner voice that insists you're never doing quite enough, never loving well enough, never healing fast enough. It disguises itself as motivation, whispering that if you just worked a little harder, spoke a little softer, gave a little more, then maybe—just maybe—you'd finally be worthy of love.

For most of us, that voice is so familiar we no longer question it. It's the soundtrack of our internal world. We call it being "realistic," being "accountable," or simply "trying to grow." But beneath those labels lies a deeply corrosive belief: that we are not enough as we are. And here's the paradox—self-criticism doesn't make us better. It makes us afraid. Afraid of failure, of rejection, of being seen too clearly. Afraid to relax into connection, because deep down, we still believe we must earn our right to belong.

This chapter marks a turning point. It invites you to revolt—not against others, but against the tyranny of your own inner judge. Because while it's true that healthy relationships require effort, boundaries, and growth, they are impossible to sustain when your primary relationship—your relationship with yourself—is built on shame.

Self-compassion is not weakness. It is not indulgence. It is the neurological and emotional foundation of all secure connection. And the science behind it is both profound and empowering.

2.1 The Neuroscience of Self-Compassion

Let's start with your brain. When you experience self-criticism—those harsh internal monologues that replay your failures, exaggerate your flaws, and predict your abandonment—your brain reacts as if you are under attack. The amygdala, your brain's fear center, lights up. Your body floods with cortisol and adrenaline. Your heart rate increases. Your muscles tense. The threat system, designed to protect you from danger, cannot tell the difference between an outside aggressor and your own thoughts. It prepares for war.

But this isn't just a momentary stress response. Over time, chronic self-criticism trains the brain into hypervigilance. It wires you to expect rejection, to distrust warmth, to anticipate abandonment even in safe relationships. It sabotages empathy—because when you're drowning in your own shame, it's hard to be truly present for someone else's needs. It erodes your capacity for emotional regulation—because your body is constantly preparing for impact.

Now contrast this with the neuroscience of self-compassion. When you respond to your own suffering with kindness, your brain activates an entirely different system: the caregiving system. This is the same network that's engaged when a parent soothes a child, or when we comfort a loved one in pain. Instead of cortisol, your body releases oxytocin—the bonding hormone. Instead of hyperarousal, your parasympathetic nervous system kicks in, creating a sense of safety. Your prefrontal cortex—the part of the brain responsible for decision-making, empathy, and perspective-taking—becomes more active. You move out of survival mode and into connection mode.

In other words, self-compassion literally changes your brain chemistry. It moves you from fear to safety, from shame to possibility. And because your nervous system is the lens through which you experience others, this shift doesn't just affect how you treat yourself—it affects how you relate to everyone around you.

Think about it. When you're stuck in self-judgment, what happens in your relationships? You become reactive, easily offended, or emotionally distant. You take things personally that aren't meant that way. You seek validation in subtle (or not-so-subtle) ways, hoping someone else will quiet the voice you refuse to soothe yourself. You overextend, overperform, or overcompensate—not out of generosity, but out of a desperate need to prove your worth.

This is not your fault. It's a learned survival mechanism. But it is your responsibility to unlearn it. Because if you want to stop reenacting your deepest wounds in your relationships, you have to start speaking to yourself differently.

Let's look at the addiction to self-criticism.

For many, being hard on themselves feels like the only path to growth. "If I'm not tough on myself," they think, "I'll get lazy, selfish, or out of control." But research paints a different picture. Studies show that self-critical individuals are *less* motivated, not more. They procrastinate more. They fear failure more. They struggle more in relationships—not because they don't care, but because they're too stuck in their own internal war to show up fully for others.

Harsh self-talk doesn't lead to excellence. It leads to paralysis.

What does drive growth? Warmth. Encouragement. Permission to make mistakes without equating them with unworthiness. This is not about excusing bad behavior or avoiding accountability. It's about creating the inner conditions necessary for real change. When you treat yourself with kindness, you're more likely to take responsibility—not less. You become more open to feedback, more resilient in the face of challenge, and more capable of repair when things go wrong.

This is what the brain needs to learn: safety is not the enemy of progress. It is its prerequisite.

And here's the most beautiful part—self-compassion doesn't stay contained. It radiates outward.

This is what psychologists call the ripple effect. When you meet your own pain with gentleness, you naturally become more compassionate toward others. You no longer need people to be perfect in order to feel safe. You stop projecting your shame onto them. You stop demanding that they reflect back your worth because you've already begun to see it for yourself.

Imagine walking into a conversation with a partner or friend— not from a place of defense or proving, but from a grounded sense of self. Imagine being able to say, "That really hurt," without making it mean *you're* unworthy or *they're* bad. Imagine having the capacity to hold both your experience and theirs without collapse. That's what self-compassion makes possible.

Because here's the truth: most relational conflict is not about what happened—it's about what it *meant*. And meaning is shaped by your internal climate. If that climate is harsh, judgmental, and hostile, even small misunderstandings feel like catastrophes. But if your inner world is compassionate, misattunements become repairable. Vulnerability becomes safe. Intimacy becomes sustainable.

This is not a linear journey. If you've spent years, even decades, using self-criticism as your motivator, this shift will feel strange at first. It may even feel dangerous. That's normal. Your nervous system is adjusting to a new rhythm. You're building new neural pathways—ones that support connection, not survival.

You might worry that self-compassion will make you complacent. That without the inner drill sergeant, you'll lose your edge. But here's what actually happens: when you remove the fear of failure, you become *bolder*, not lazier. You take more emotional risks, because you know you can survive the outcome. You stop walking on eggshells in your relationships. You stop trying to be perfect, and start trying to be real.

And that's where the magic lives. In the authenticity that compassion allows.

To live this way—to choose kindness over criticism, again and again—is a revolution. Not in the dramatic sense, but in the quiet, powerful, soul-altering sense. It's a revolution against every voice that told you love had to be earned. Against every belief that said you were only as good as your performance. Against every internalized message that made you fear your own humanity.

It's not an easy revolution. But it is a necessary one. And its effects ripple out far beyond your personal well-being.

Because when you treat yourself with compassion, you become the kind of person who can hold others with grace. You stop reacting from woundedness. You stop projecting your worth onto your partner's attention or your friend's approval. You bring stability into your relationships—not the brittle kind that demands control, but the flexible, resilient kind that bends and grows and holds space for imperfection.

The science is clear. The path is evident. And the choice is yours.

You can keep living in the tyranny of self-judgment, hoping that shame will sculpt you into someone more lovable. Or you can choose to step into a new way of being—one where growth is fueled by gentleness, not fear. One where your brain, your heart, and your relationships are all guided by the quiet power of compassion.

Because you do not have to earn your worth. You only have to stop forgetting it.

And in remembering, everything changes.

2.2 Healing the Inner Critic's Impact on Love

There is no greater saboteur of intimacy than the voice inside you insisting that you must earn the right to be loved. This inner critic—silent to the outside world but deafening within—convinces you that unless you are perfect, agreeable, in control, or emotionally composed, you are not worthy of connection. The cost of this voice is enormous. It's not just internal stress or self-doubt. It's the deep loneliness that comes from never truly being seen—not because others refuse to see you, but because you keep hiding behind the mask your critic demands you wear.

For many, the most deceptive disguise of the inner critic is perfectionism. On the surface, it looks admirable: responsibility, ambition, high standards. But in the realm of relationships, perfectionism is a barrier—not a bridge. It tells you that vulnerability is dangerous, that mistakes are unacceptable, that your emotions must be tidy and manageable before they can be shared. The result is a version of yourself that might look polished, but feels hollow. You may say all the right things, anticipate every possible emotional reaction, offer support with precision—but behind it all, there's a quiet desperation to be enough.

This is the perfectionism-intimacy paradox: the harder you try to be perfect, the harder it becomes to be close. Authentic intimacy requires presence, not performance. It thrives on uncertainty, on messiness, on moments where you say the wrong thing and trust the relationship is strong enough to hold it. But when your inner critic has taught you that mistakes equal rejection, you become emotionally armored. You choose control over closeness, composure over connection. You may even convince yourself that you are safer alone, that love is too risky unless you can guarantee its outcome. And yet, in that pursuit of safety, you sacrifice the very aliveness that makes love meaningful.

If perfectionism is the armor, people-pleasing is the disguise. It's one of the inner critic's most cunning strategies—because it masquerades as kindness. But when you examine it closely, people-pleasing is not about generosity; it's about survival. It's the learned behavior of someone who has equated approval with safety. Someone who has internalized the message that their needs are secondary, their emotions are burdensome, and their worth depends on how well they keep others comfortable.

The tragedy of people-pleasing is that it breeds disconnection even as it seeks closeness. By constantly molding yourself to fit others' expectations, you deny them the chance to know who you truly are. You silence your desires, minimize your discomfort, tolerate what wounds you—all in the name of being liked. But intimacy cannot flourish in pretense. Love cannot take root in a version of you that doesn't exist. And over time, people-pleasing breeds resentment—not just toward those you bend for, but toward yourself, for continually abandoning your own needs.

This abandonment may feel subtle at first. A hesitated truth. A smile when you wanted to cry. A yes when your body screamed no. But the accumulation of these moments tells your nervous system something dangerous: *your truth is not welcome here.* And when that belief calcifies, it becomes very hard to stay open, even in the presence of someone loving.

Perhaps the most painful consequence of self-criticism in relationships is emotional unavailability—not because you don't care, but because you're too afraid to stay. When the critic inside flares up during conflict or disappointment, it floods the system with shame. And shame, unlike guilt, doesn't say *I did something wrong*—it says *I am something wrong.* That distinction is crucial, because shame doesn't inspire repair. It inspires collapse.

In the grip of shame, you may shut down or lash out. You might retreat behind silence or defensiveness. You may feel the urgent need to fix everything or prove your worth, not because the other person is asking you to, but because the critic has already decided that you are the problem. This creates a tragic loop: something goes wrong, you feel inadequate, you withdraw or attack, and the rupture deepens. What could have been a moment of connection—of working through pain together—becomes another confirmation of your unworthiness.

To interrupt this loop, you need a different kind of skill: shame resilience. This is not about never feeling shame; it's about staying in connection even when you do. It's the ability to say, "I'm hurting, and I want to stay with you in this." It's knowing that your flaws don't make you unlovable. That your emotions, even when messy, are not too much. That your humanity is not a liability in love—it's the very condition that makes love possible.

Healing the inner critic is not about silencing it entirely. That voice was built to protect you. It believed that if it could control your every move, you might avoid rejection. It tried to earn for you the love you didn't know how to receive. But now, its methods are outdated. You don't need to fight it. You need to outgrow it. To meet it with curiosity instead of obedience. To hear its fear without making it your guide.

This is a slow, layered process. But every time you choose truth over perfection, boundaries over appeasement, connection over self-protection, you reclaim a piece of yourself. You begin to create a love that is spacious enough to hold your wholeness— not just the polished parts, but the trembling, tender, beautifully human ones too.

2.3 Practices for Embodied Self-Acceptance

If the previous chapter was about understanding the inner critic and its impact, this one is about rewriting the script—concretely, slowly, and in the body. Because self-acceptance cannot be achieved through intellect alone. You can't out-think shame. You can't logic your way into wholeness. You have to *feel* it. You have to create, in real time, a relationship with yourself that mirrors the love you've always craved.

One of the most profound ways to begin this transformation is through what might be called the loving witness practice. This is not a technique you perform; it's a relationship you build—between the part of you that struggles and the part of you that can hold that struggle with gentleness. Most of us have developed a harsh internal observer, trained by years of criticism and comparison. The loving witness is different. It doesn't rush to correct or fix. It simply *sees*—with presence, warmth, and an open heart.

When you make a mistake, instead of spiraling into self-condemnation, you pause and observe: *Ah, I see I'm hurting. I see I just reacted from fear. I see I'm caught in a familiar story.* And then you stay. You don't abandon yourself. You don't drown in the feeling. You just sit with it, the way you would with a crying child. This presence—simple, steady, kind—is one of the most transformative forces in your emotional life.

Over time, as this internal relationship deepens, you begin to develop what some call the "inner parent"—a part of you that can provide what you may never have consistently received: emotional safety, validation, attunement. This is the heart of reparenting your relational self. It means no longer waiting for someone else to give you the love you lacked, and instead learning how to offer it to yourself. Not to replace external love, but to stop needing it to prove your worth.

Reparenting is not about indulgence. It's about structure. It's about knowing when to comfort yourself and when to challenge yourself. When to say, *You're doing your best, and that's enough,* and when to say, *I know this feels hard, but we can do it anyway.*

It's learning to listen to your inner world with discernment, not dismissal. To honor your boundaries. To track your nervous system. To know when you need rest, movement, silence, or connection.

This kind of self-relationship doesn't happen overnight. It's built in small moments—in the way you speak to yourself in the mirror, in the way you respond to disappointment, in the pauses between conflict and reaction. Every choice to be gentle with yourself is a brick in the foundation of a new internal home.

And then there is forgiveness. Not as a one-time act, but as a daily practice. Most of us carry a silent weight: the relationships we ruined, the moments we ghosted, the lies we told to be liked, the times we stayed when we should've left or left when we should've stayed. We replay these memories not to learn from them, but to punish ourselves. As if carrying the guilt will somehow redeem us.

But guilt is not penance. It's a doorway. Forgiveness means walking through it—not to forget what happened, but to learn from it with tenderness. To say, *Yes, I hurt someone. And yes, I was doing the best I could with what I knew.* This doesn't excuse harm, but it releases you from the prison of perpetual regret. Because regret, when held too tightly, becomes identity. And identity built on shame cannot hold love.

To forgive yourself is not to minimize your impact. It's to acknowledge it *and* commit to doing better—not from self-loathing, but from self-respect. To say, *I am worthy of love, even as I grow.* This is not easy. But it is sacred. It is the quiet, radical act of making peace with your past so you can live fully in your present.

Embodied self-acceptance is not a destination. It's a rhythm. Some days you will fall back into criticism, collapse into people-pleasing, armor yourself in perfection. That's okay. The goal is not to be perfect. The goal is to notice when you leave yourself—and come back sooner. With less judgment. With more grace.

Because every time you return to yourself with love, you become more available for real intimacy. You become someone who can hold space—not just for your own complexity, but for another's. You stop demanding perfection from yourself, and therefore stop needing it from others. You begin to love in a way that liberates, not binds. That sees clearly, not conditionally.

And from that place, relationships change—not because others do, but because you are finally home in yourself. And from that home, love flows. Freely. Fully. Unafraid.

Chapter 3: The Art of Emotional Alchemy – Transforming Difficult Feelings into Relationship Gold

"The cave you fear to enter holds the treasure you seek." – *Joseph Campbell*

3.1 Befriending Your Emotional Landscape

Most of us have been conditioned to treat our emotions like intruders. We welcome joy, excitement, and affection at the front door, but sadness must knock twice before it's let in. Anger gets told to stay outside. Fear is shuffled into a closet. And shame— we pretend we don't even live in the same house. Yet these are the very visitors who carry the deepest wisdom. They arrive, not to harm us, but to illuminate what we haven't yet faced. The art of emotional alchemy begins when we stop resisting our feelings and start listening to them. Not just passively, but with curiosity and reverence—as messengers sent from the deepest corners of our psyche.

Most people don't have a relationship with their emotions. They have reactions to them. When sadness surfaces, they distract. When anger bubbles up, they suppress. When anxiety spikes, they race for solutions. But an emotionally mature life asks for something different. It asks you to stay. To lean in. To get quiet enough to hear what that feeling is trying to say before you bury it or act it out. Emotions are not obstacles on the path to intimacy—they *are* the path. They are the language of the soul, the invisible tether that connects our internal world to those around us.

At the core of emotional alchemy is a shift in perception. Feelings are not problems to be fixed. They are information systems. When you feel angry, your body is signaling that something you value has been crossed or threatened. When you feel sad, your heart is telling you something matters deeply—perhaps something has been lost, or is aching to be acknowledged. When anxiety rises, it's not because you're broken, but because something inside you senses unpredictability, danger, or a lack of safety. And when you ignore or override these messages, you don't become stronger. You become disconnected—from yourself and from the people who matter most.

The truth is, emotional fluency is what separates reactive relationships from resilient ones. When two people can recognize their own emotional signals, communicate them clearly, and honor each other's emotional experience without trying to fix or avoid it, intimacy deepens. But if you don't know what you're feeling—if everything inside you gets labeled "bad" or "too much"—then the people around you don't get to meet the real you. They meet your defenses. Your withdrawal. Your appeasement. Your anger without context. And the chance for true connection slips through the cracks.

Developing a relationship with your emotional landscape requires slowing down. It asks you to stop moving past your feelings and start moving *with* them. Instead of thinking, "I'm just overwhelmed," you learn to name what kind of overwhelmed. Is it helplessness? Is it overstimulation? Is it grief masked as frustration? These distinctions matter. Because when you can name your experience precisely, you can respond with precision. Emotional granularity is not a luxury of poets—it is a survival skill in love.

Think of how many arguments arise not from what was said, but from the emotions underneath what wasn't said. A partner lashes out—not because they're cruel, but because they felt dismissed.

A friend pulls away—not because they don't care, but because they didn't know how to voice their disappointment. Parents, lovers, colleagues—all speaking over each other's emotional heads because no one was taught the language of nuance. Because "I'm fine" is easier than "I feel abandoned, and I'm scared to tell you that."

Emotional granularity means having more than five crayons in your emotional box. Not just sad, angry, happy, anxious, or numb—but curious, tender, disillusioned, betrayed, exhilarated, ashamed, soothed, proud, lonely. When your inner vocabulary expands, your outer world becomes more navigable. You stop reacting in extremes. You start responding in layers. And in that shift, relationships become less about fixing problems and more about witnessing each other in truth.

But before you can develop this skill with another, you have to cultivate it within yourself. That means learning to sit with discomfort. To say, "Something's stirring in me. I don't need to rush it away. I don't need to make it look better. I just need to *be* with it." It means remembering that no emotion is permanent—and that every emotion, if fully felt, will move. Not always fast. Not always neatly. But movement is its nature. Suppression creates stagnation. Expression creates flow.

Still, expressing doesn't mean unloading. It doesn't mean acting out every feeling as soon as it arrives. It means honoring the message without making it your master. It means asking, "What is this emotion asking of me?" before deciding how—or whether—to act on it. Sometimes sadness asks you to grieve. Sometimes it asks you to rest. Sometimes it asks for connection. Emotional intelligence is knowing the difference.

And this is where emotional alchemy earns its name. Alchemy, in its essence, is the transformation of something raw and dense into something luminous and refined. In this context, it's about taking the lead of our pain—the heaviness, the fear, the stuckness—and turning it into insight, clarity, even compassion. Not through denial, but through deep presence. Through trusting that on the other side of every difficult feeling is a deeper truth that wants to be seen.

For example, anger is so often demonized, especially in people who were raised to believe that expressing frustration is dangerous, impolite, or shameful. But anger is not the enemy. It's a boundary defender. A clarifier. It says, "Something here needs attention." The task is not to extinguish anger, but to learn how to hear it without being consumed by it. To trace it back to its root—Was it a betrayal? A crossed value? A loss of control?—and then choose a response that honors the wisdom without harming the connection.

Anxiety is another misunderstood guide. Often pathologized, medicated, or dismissed, it is rarely approached as a signal worth listening to. But anxiety, when examined with gentleness, almost always points to something sacred. A need for stability. A desire for reassurance. A longing for control in a world that offers little. The goal is not to rid yourself of anxiety, but to develop a relationship with it. To understand what soothes it. What feeds it. What grounds it. In doing so, you begin to live from clarity, not reactivity.

Sadness, too, is a powerful teacher. In a culture that idolizes positivity and productivity, sadness is often seen as failure. But sadness is the emotional glue that binds us to meaning. You don't grieve what you don't care about. To feel sadness fully is to acknowledge the depth of your connection—to people, to dreams, to memories. It is not weakness. It is reverence. And when honored, it softens the heart, not hardens it.

Of course, none of this is easy. Especially if you grew up in an environment where emotions were unsafe, ridiculed, or ignored.

In such environments, children learn to disconnect from their bodies as a survival strategy. They learn to read the room before they read themselves. They become attuned to others' moods while remaining strangers to their own. Reclaiming your emotional self in adulthood, then, is an act of reclamation. It is slow. It is tender. And it is revolutionary.

Start by noticing. Noticing when you're uncomfortable and wanting to check your phone. When you're agitated and feel the urge to lash out. When you're lonely but pretend you're just tired. These moments are gateways. If you pause and breathe into them—literally breathe—you create a crack in the wall of unconscious reaction. In that crack, new choices emerge. You might realize you're not angry, but afraid. Not distant, but vulnerable. And in that realization, a deeper truth becomes available—not just to you, but to anyone who loves you.

This is emotional alchemy: not controlling your emotions, but collaborating with them. Not spiritualizing your pain, but dignifying it. Seeing every feeling as a thread in the tapestry of your humanity, and choosing—again and again—to follow that thread until it leads to something gold.

Because the cave you fear to enter—whether it's sadness, shame, or anger—holds the treasure you seek: connection, authenticity, peace. The ability to stay with yourself through the full range of experience without splintering, and in doing so, to offer that same unwavering presence to another. This is the work. This is the art. And it begins, always, with the courage to feel.

3.2 The Container for Feeling

Most people are not taught how to feel. They are taught how to fix, how to hide, how to repress, how to explain, and how to distract. But true healing and intimacy require something different: the ability to sit with raw emotion—unfiltered, unsolved, unapologetic—and allow it to move through the body without becoming consumed or overwhelmed by it. This is the essence of emotional containment. It is not about suppression, nor is it about eruption. It is about creating an internal space large enough, strong enough, and kind enough to hold your most intense experiences with steadiness.

Imagine a glass of water. If you pour boiling water into a small, delicate glass, it shatters. But if you pour that same boiling water into a large, sturdy container, it holds without breaking. Your emotional body works the same way. Without a resilient inner container, intense emotions like anger, fear, grief, or shame can fracture your relationships and disrupt your sense of self. They spill outward in blame, manipulation, withdrawal, or impulsivity—not because you are broken, but because you've never been given the tools to hold what hurts without needing to offload it.

Emotional resilience is not the absence of pain—it is the capacity to stay present with it. To feel the burn of anger in your chest and choose not to lash out. To feel the hollow ache of sadness and not immediately rush into distraction. To feel the sting of rejection and resist the urge to armor up or retaliate. This is the real work of maturity—not perfection, but presence. The ability to remain in contact with yourself long enough for the emotion to reveal what it came to teach you.

This doesn't mean staying stuck in difficult feelings. It means *staying with* them just long enough to listen. Every emotion has a voice, and it speaks not in logic but in sensation. The tight jaw, the racing heart, the flushed cheeks—these are not nuisances to ignore; they are signals. They are the body's language, asking you to slow down, to turn inward, to attend.

And here's the crucial skill: learning how to *pause*.

Between the moment you feel something and the moment you respond, there is a window. In that window lives your freedom. Most people live in such a contracted state that the window is milliseconds wide. Someone criticizes you, and you snap. Your partner forgets something important, and your stomach drops, followed immediately by silence or sarcasm. That tiny sliver between stimulus and response is where all transformation begins. And the more you practice widening it, the more empowered you become—not because you suppress your emotions, but because you own them.

This space—this pause—is where emotional sovereignty is born. It gives you room to notice the story you're telling yourself, to feel the old wounds being reactivated, to ask yourself, *Is this about now, or is this about then?* In that pause, you can regulate your nervous system, choose your words with care, and respond in alignment with who you want to be, rather than who your pain wants you to become.

Of course, this requires practice. Because when you're triggered, your body doesn't want to pause. It wants to act. The fight-or-flight response doesn't wait for permission—it floods you. Your amygdala, the part of your brain that scans for threat, overrides your logical thinking. Your heart rate spikes, your breath shortens, your muscles prepare for defense or escape. This is not a moral failing. It is biology.

The challenge, then, is not to eliminate the stress response, but to work with it. To develop techniques that signal to your body: *You are safe. You don't need to fight. You don't need to run. You can stay here, and feel.* This is where nervous system regulation becomes essential—not just for your own well-being, but for the health of every relationship you hold.

Simple but profound practices can help. Breathwork that extends the exhale signals safety. Grounding techniques—like placing your hands on your heart or thighs, pressing your feet into the ground, naming things you can see—anchor you in the present moment. Humming, gentle swaying, or even placing a warm hand on your abdomen can stimulate the vagus nerve, helping shift your system from sympathetic arousal to the parasympathetic, socially engaged "ventral vagal" state. This state is not passive—it is the optimal condition for clear thinking, emotional regulation, and connected communication.

The more you practice these tools outside of conflict, the more accessible they become when you need them. They build muscle memory in your nervous system, gradually increasing your window of tolerance. Over time, situations that once felt intolerable become manageable. You learn that you can survive intensity without outsourcing it. You can feel fully without collapsing or harming. This is the container. This is what allows you to meet life with presence.

And here's the paradox: the stronger your internal container, the softer you become. Not weak, but available. Because you're no longer bracing against your own inner world. You're no longer terrified of what might surface. You trust your capacity to hold. To witness. To metabolize. And that trust radiates. People feel it. They feel safer around you—not because you're always calm, but because you're not ruled by your reactivity.

This kind of self-possession transforms relationships. Conflicts de-escalate more quickly. Emotional honesty becomes less threatening. Boundaries are drawn not from panic, but from clarity. You stop waiting for others to regulate you. You stop needing every emotional discomfort to be soothed by someone else. And ironically, this makes you even more available for connection—not less.

You become someone who can stay. With yourself. With another. With life. And in that staying, something sacred unfolds.

3.3 Emotional Transparency and Authentic Sharing

There is a moment in every relationship—whether romantic, familial, or platonic—where one person hesitates. They feel something strong: grief, jealousy, fear, rage, tenderness. And they wonder: *Should I say this? Should I let them in? Will they get it? Will it be too much?*

That moment is a turning point. If the emotion is withheld, it simmers. If it's expressed carelessly, it can wound. But if it's shared with clarity, responsibility, and timing, it can deepen intimacy in a way few other things can. Emotional transparency is not just about telling the truth—it's about how, when, and why you tell it.

To begin, it's essential to understand the difference between sharing and emotional dumping. Sharing invites connection. Dumping demands relief. Sharing says, *Here's what I'm feeling, and I want to bring you into it.* Dumping says, *I need to unload this on you because I don't know how to hold it myself.*

When you share with awareness, you stay rooted in your own experience. You don't make the other person responsible for your feelings. You don't use your emotions to manipulate, punish, or control. You speak from the center of yourself, not from your edges. You say, *I'm feeling afraid because I care,* not *You're making me feel unsafe.* You say, *I'm feeling overwhelmed and could use support,* not *You never show up for me.*

This kind of communication requires practice. It requires knowing your own internal state well enough to articulate it without blame. It also requires developing the courage to speak vulnerably without certainty of outcome. Because real emotional transparency does not guarantee the other person will meet you there. It simply offers the invitation.

Timing and context matter deeply. There is a difference between honesty and impulsivity. Sharing a deep wound in the middle of an argument rarely creates understanding. Expressing fear just as someone walks out the door is not vulnerability—it's panic. Part of emotional intelligence is knowing when the soil is fertile for truth. When the other person is receptive, regulated, and available. That doesn't mean waiting for perfect conditions. It means honoring the moment as much as the message.

Creating this sensitivity means checking in with yourself first: *What do I actually want from this conversation? Do I want to be understood? To connect? To ask for something specific? Or am I just looking to discharge emotion I haven't processed yet?* That self-inquiry is not about silencing yourself. It's about aligning your words with your intention.

Taking responsibility for your emotional world doesn't mean isolating or bottling up your pain. It means recognizing that your feelings are yours—even when they're triggered by someone else. You can own your sadness without making the other person feel guilty. You can express anger without attacking. You can name disappointment without dramatizing. This level of ownership creates safety. It tells the other person: *I'm not here to blame you. I'm here to be real with you.*

This is how mature emotional sharing differs from raw reactivity. One connects. The other divides. One opens doors. The other slams them.

When you develop the ability to share from a grounded place, relationships change. Defenses soften. Curiosity replaces defensiveness. Empathy flows more easily. Because the truth is, people aren't scared of your emotions. They're scared of how you handle them. If your sadness becomes accusation, or your anger becomes control, they will shut down. But if you stay rooted in your own experience—if you share cleanly, bravely, clearly—they will lean in.

The goal isn't to be perfectly composed. The goal is to be real, without needing to explode or collapse. To let someone see you—not your strategies, not your coping, but *you*. That kind of honesty is magnetic. It invites others into their own authenticity. It creates a field where masks fall away, and two people meet—not as polished versions of themselves, but as whole, evolving humans.

Emotional transparency is a dance. It asks you to feel deeply, speak carefully, and remain open to how the other person responds. It's not always graceful. But it's always generative.

Because when we share truthfully—when we let someone into our inner weather without asking them to fix the storm—we create the conditions for love to grow not on the surface, but at the roots. Not just in moments of ease, but in moments of depth.

And that is what real intimacy is made of.

Chapter 4: The Dance of Boundaries – Creating Sacred Space for Authentic Connection

Healthy relationships do not require merging into one another. They require room to breathe. Yet many of us confuse closeness with collapse, intimacy with enmeshment, and love with self-sacrifice. We are taught—through culture, family, or lived experience—that loving someone means giving everything, saying yes even when we mean no, and accommodating until we disappear. But the truth is, without boundaries, there can be no real connection. Only codependence, resentment, and emotional exhaustion disguised as devotion.

Boundaries are not barriers. They are bridges. They are the sacred agreements we make with ourselves and with others that allow us to stay true, rooted, and open at the same time. They are not about keeping people out—they are about keeping ourselves *in*. In alignment. In integrity. In relationship with who we truly are.

When people hear the word "boundary," they often think of conflict. Of saying no. Of confrontation. But boundaries are not inherently harsh. They are not rigid walls or cold ultimatums. At their best, boundaries are acts of love—toward self *and* others. They say, "This is where I end and you begin," not because I don't care, but because I care enough to show up as my whole self, not as a fragmented version built to please or appease.

We often mistake boundaries for control. But control is about trying to manage other people's behavior, emotions, or choices. Boundaries are about managing *yourself*. The distinction is subtle but vital. If you say, "You can't talk to me that way," with the unspoken goal of changing the other person, you're in control mode. But if you say, "If I'm spoken to that way, I will remove myself from the conversation," you're in boundary territory. One is about force. The other is about clarity.

This is the difference between external and internal boundaries. External boundaries aim to shape the outside world, often from a place of fear. Internal boundaries begin with an honest look inward. They ask, *What am I willing to tolerate? What honors my values? What preserves my peace?* And from that clarity, a line is drawn—not to divide, but to define. To declare where your responsibility ends and where someone else's begins.

Boundaries don't disconnect us. They make connection safe. They signal that we are self-aware enough to name our limits and emotionally literate enough to honor others' limits too. Without boundaries, we become inconsistent. We say yes and then resent it. We smile while we're shrinking. We show up physically but check out emotionally. Over time, those patterns erode trust—not just with others, but within ourselves.

The irony is that many people who avoid setting boundaries do so because they fear rejection or conflict. But in avoiding those difficult moments, they create far more suffering in the long run. They stretch themselves thin, then snap. They swallow their truth, then explode. They say yes while their entire nervous system screams no. And eventually, relationships suffer—not because there wasn't love, but because there wasn't structure. Because there was no container strong enough to hold the full truth of each person involved.

Setting boundaries is not selfish. It's self-respecting. It says, "I know what I need to stay in connection without abandoning myself." That might mean needing space after a hard conversation. It might mean limiting certain topics with certain people. It might mean carving out time for solitude, or refusing to engage in toxic dynamics. But each boundary set from self-awareness builds a stronger foundation for the relationship to rest on. Not a house of illusions, but a home of honesty.

Of course, boundaries are not always easy to communicate. Especially if you were raised to prioritize harmony over truth, or if your past boundaries were punished, mocked, or ignored. In such cases, boundary-setting can feel like betrayal. Like cruelty. But discomfort does not mean you're doing it wrong. It often means you're doing it for the first time.

The way you communicate a boundary matters. Boundaries delivered with shame or superiority often create defensiveness. But boundaries expressed with grounded clarity and emotional transparency create possibility. They say, "Here's what I need to remain in connection with you." They say, "I want to stay close, and this is how I can do that authentically."

The goal is not to create distance, but to sustain presence. To say no with kindness. To say yes with integrity. To create conditions in which both people can stay in the room—not out of obligation, but from choice.

This is where the flexibility paradox comes in. Most people assume that having boundaries means being rigid. But in reality, clear boundaries are what make flexibility possible. When you know your limits, you can play within them. You can be spontaneous, generous, emotionally available—because you're not secretly calculating how much more you can take before you burn out. You're not giving from a place of depletion. You're not constantly scanning for danger. You're anchored.

Think of a river. If it has no banks, it floods. If its banks are too narrow, it stagnates. But with strong, steady banks, the river flows with power and direction. Your boundaries are the banks. They give your emotional life shape and movement. They prevent you from losing yourself in others, or asking others to lose themselves in you. They create a rhythm—of closeness and space, of yes and no—that allows love to move freely without overwhelm or collapse.

In this dance, boundaries are not static. They evolve. A boundary that served you five years ago might now be a wall. A line you couldn't draw before might now be essential. Relationships breathe when boundaries breathe. When they're checked in on, revised, honored. When both people feel safe enough to say, "This isn't working for me anymore. Can we talk about it?"

This is how boundaries become relational, not just personal. Not "my way or the highway," but "here's what's true for me— what's true for you?" Not rules to follow, but values to uphold. In this way, boundaries become collaborative. They become invitations into deeper understanding, not threats of disconnection.

Of course, some people won't like your boundaries. Especially those who benefited from your lack of them. When you begin to say no, when you stop over-functioning, when you step back from roles you never agreed to carry—there may be resistance. That's okay. You're not responsible for others' reactions to your truth. You're responsible for speaking it with love. For holding it with grace. For staying rooted when the wind of disapproval blows.

This takes courage. But every time you honor a boundary, you build trust with yourself. You prove that your needs matter. That your values are real. That your presence is not a performance— it's a choice.

And slowly, the people around you learn: when you say yes, it's because you mean it. When you show up, it's because you want to. When you love, it's because you're free to—not because you're afraid not to.

That is the power of boundaries. They transform love from obligation into liberation. They take relationships from guessing games into grounded clarity. They allow two whole people to meet, not as rescuers or performers, but as partners. As mirrors. As fellow travelers on the path of truth.

In the chapters to come, we'll explore what it means to hold boundaries in moments of rupture, how to navigate boundaries in layered dynamics—family, work, romance—and how to repair when boundaries are crossed. But for now, the invitation is simple: begin to feel where your edges are. Where you contract. Where you give too much. Where you stay too long.

And then ask yourself: *What would it mean to protect this part of me—not with a wall, but with a promise? Not with anger, but with clarity? Not to push someone away, but to stay close without disappearing?*

That is the dance. That is the art. That is the sacred work of love.

4.2 The Energetic Dimension of Boundaries

Boundaries are not only about words and actions. Long before a line is drawn or a limit is spoken, boundaries exist on an energetic level. They are felt in the body, sensed in the nervous system, and communicated in the subtle ways we lean in or pull away. You can be sitting in silence with someone and still feel overwhelmed, invaded, or unseen. You can be physically apart from someone and still feel tethered by obligation, guilt, or unresolved emotional entanglement. This is the often overlooked, yet profoundly important, energetic dimension of boundaries.

Energy moves between people. This is not a metaphor—it is a reality most of us experience but rarely name. When you walk into a room and feel drained without speaking a word, when a conversation leaves you feeling heavy for hours afterward, when you can't stop thinking about someone else's problem even though it has nothing to do with your life—these are signs of energetic enmeshment. It happens when your emotional field becomes porous, when your empathy becomes overextension, when connection becomes entanglement.

Energetic enmeshment often masquerades as care. It sounds like "I'm just being supportive," or "I don't want to let them down," but beneath it lies a deeper unconscious contract: *If I carry your pain, maybe you'll love me. If I shrink myself, maybe you'll stay. If I take responsibility for your emotions, maybe I'll be safe.* This pattern frequently begins in childhood, particularly in families where emotional needs were inconsistent, unspoken, or placed on the child to meet. Over time, you learn to scan others constantly, to anticipate moods, to emotionally shape-shift as a survival strategy. But what helps you survive in childhood often stifles you in adulthood.

In close relationships, this energetic merging can feel like intimacy at first. You feel close, intertwined, needed. But over time, it suffocates. You stop knowing where you end and the other begins. You say yes when your body wants to say no. You feel anxiety when they're upset, not because they've told you, but because your whole system is wired to tune into others before tuning into yourself. And eventually, you begin to disappear.

True connection is not the dissolving of self—it's the honoring of two selves meeting with clarity. Sovereignty within intimacy means you can love someone deeply without absorbing their every emotion. You can hold space for their process without losing access to your own truth. You can be present with someone's disappointment without collapsing into guilt or shame.

This requires cultivating awareness of your own energetic space. It begins with noticing how you feel around different people—not just emotionally, but physically. Do you tense when a certain person texts you? Do you feel drained after a conversation? Do you find yourself replaying arguments or trying to solve problems that don't belong to you? These are signs that your energetic boundaries have become blurred.

The practice of energetic sovereignty involves re-centering yourself regularly. It means learning to come back to your own breath, your own body, your own thoughts. Not to disconnect from others, but to stay anchored in yourself as you relate to them. This is not coldness. It is clarity. You are able to show up with compassion because you're not drowning in someone else's waves.

One of the most powerful, yet often unspoken, challenges in maintaining energetic boundaries is the moment when someone reacts negatively to your self-protection. When someone becomes angry because you won't drop everything for them. When someone uses guilt to try to pull you back into an old pattern. When someone calls you selfish for simply taking care of yourself. This is the moment when many people fold. They second-guess their needs. They doubt their boundaries. They retreat from their truth in order to restore peace.

But this is where the art of non-violent resistance becomes essential. Non-violent resistance means holding your ground without hostility. It means staying rooted in your values, your limits, your truth—even when someone else doesn't like it. It is the decision to honor yourself without needing to defend or attack. To say no without explanation. To walk away without malice. To let someone be upset without making it your job to soothe them.

This doesn't mean you become unfeeling or rigid. It means you stop abandoning yourself to manage other people's emotional responses. You trust that their discomfort is not a sign that you've done something wrong. It's often a sign that you've changed—and that change threatens a dynamic they may not be ready to let go of.

But growth requires discomfort. Not cruelty, not coldness—but the willingness to let things shift, stretch, or even rupture when necessary. Your task is not to control how others feel about your boundaries. Your task is to stay true to yourself with as much integrity and compassion as you can muster.

Energetic boundaries are not fixed. They are dynamic and responsive. They require you to stay attuned—not only to others, but to yourself. When you feel overwhelmed, it's a cue to pause, to recalibrate, to return to center. When you feel resentment brewing, it's a sign that something needs to be voiced. When you feel disconnected, it may be time to open more—not necessarily to others, but first to yourself.

Ultimately, the energetic work of boundaries is the inner commitment to stay in right relationship with your own nervous system, your own truth, and your own aliveness. It is the steady returning to self, again and again, so that you can meet others not from depletion or desperation, but from fullness. From choice. From love—not the kind that swallows you, but the kind that liberates you.

4.3 Boundaries with Different Relationship Types

There is no one-size-fits-all when it comes to boundaries. While the core principles—self-respect, clarity, sovereignty—remain consistent, the application of those principles must be flexible. Each relationship demands a different tone, texture, and level of intimacy. A boundary with a parent is not the same as a boundary with a colleague, nor is it the same as one with a romantic partner. The art lies in customizing your boundaries to suit the context while staying anchored in who you are.

Family boundaries are often the most layered and emotionally charged. These relationships are steeped in history, loyalty, cultural norms, and unspoken expectations. Many people feel torn between the desire for autonomy and the fear of betraying their family. In enmeshed family systems, it can feel nearly impossible to assert independence without triggering guilt or disapproval. There is often an unspoken rule that says: we stay close, even if it costs us our individuality.

Breaking that rule can be painful—but also essential. Adult autonomy does not mean cutting ties or rejecting your family. It means re-negotiating the terms of the relationship so that you can show up authentically. That might mean setting time limits on certain interactions, declining invitations that drain you, or choosing not to engage in cycles of dysfunction that you've outgrown. It might mean saying, "I love you, and I'm not available for this conversation," or "I care about our relationship, which is why I need some space to breathe."

The key is to anchor your boundaries in love rather than rebellion. Not, "You always control me, so I'm cutting you off," but "I'm learning how to take care of myself, and I need a little more space to do that." When boundaries are set from love, they become less threatening. They invite dialogue, rather than defensiveness. And even if your family doesn't understand them right away, you'll know you're acting from alignment—not reactivity.

Professional boundaries require a different kind of finesse. The workplace is often filled with invisible power dynamics, unspoken expectations, and blurred lines between professionalism and personal connection. It can be tempting to overextend, to people-please, or to stay silent in the face of inappropriate behavior for fear of rocking the boat. But healthy work boundaries are essential—not just for your well-being, but for your effectiveness.

This doesn't mean becoming distant or rigid. You can bring warmth, authenticity, and collaboration to your work relationships while still protecting your time, your energy, and your integrity. It means knowing when to say no to extra responsibilities that aren't yours. It means keeping personal disclosures within limits that feel safe. It means stepping back when you notice yourself absorbing others' stress or over-identifying with roles that don't belong to you.

Boundaries at work also require clarity—both internal and external. Internally, you need to be clear about what you value, what you're willing to compromise on, and where your non-negotiables lie. Externally, you need to communicate those clearly, whether through your actions, your calendar, or your direct communication. The more consistent you are, the less confusion there is. The more you model healthy boundaries, the more permission you give others to do the same.

In intimate partnerships, boundaries can feel paradoxical. Many people believe that love means full access—that if someone loves you, they should want to know everything, be with you constantly, and share every emotion. But this myth of romantic fusion is not intimacy. It is emotional over-dependence dressed up as closeness.

Real intimacy flourishes in space. When you have clear boundaries in a romantic relationship, you create the conditions for desire, respect, and authenticity to thrive. You are able to say, "I need time alone," without fear of punishment. You can disagree without fear of abandonment. You can ask for what you want without feeling selfish or needy.

These boundaries may involve how you spend your time, how you navigate conflict, how much emotional labor you take on, how you handle shared finances or household responsibilities. But they all share the same root: the recognition that two separate people are choosing each other—not out of obligation, but from sovereignty.

When you maintain your individuality in partnership, you actually increase your capacity for connection. You're not relating from emptiness, but from wholeness. You're not clinging, but choosing. And in that choosing, intimacy becomes not something you fall into, but something you co-create.

Boundaries across relationship types are not about distancing—they are about defining. They define who you are, what you value, and how you want to be treated. And they invite others to meet you there—not in perfection, but in presence. Not in conformity, but in respect.

Ultimately, boundary work is about self-leadership. It's the decision to live from the inside out—to let your values, your truth, and your integrity guide how you show up, rather than letting guilt, fear, or external pressure dictate your behavior.

As you continue walking this path, remember: boundaries are not once-and-done declarations. They are living conversations. They evolve. They get tested. They require courage. But each time you honor them, you come home to yourself a little more. And from that home, you build relationships that are not just connected—but free.

Chapter 5: The Language of the Heart – Communication That Creates Connection

"The single biggest problem in communication is the illusion that it has taken place." – George Bernard Shaw

5.1 Beyond Words – The Multilayered Nature of Communication

We often think that communication is about words—about what we say, how we say it, and whether or not the other person agrees. But the heart knows otherwise. Anyone who has ever sat through a conversation where "everything sounded fine" but felt inexplicably tense, or heard an "I'm okay" that rang hollow, or sensed withdrawal behind a smile, knows that what's said is often the smallest part of what's actually being communicated. In relationships, it's not just about the content. It's about the current beneath the words—the energy, the tone, the timing, the presence. The silent language that speaks volumes even when no one's talking.

Human communication is a symphony of layers, with words playing only a minor role. The psychologist Albert Mehrabian's famous 55-38-7 formula is often cited for a reason: only 7% of our communication is verbal. The rest—93%—is a blend of vocal tone and body language. While this isn't a universal rule, especially in complex discussions or written dialogue, it still reveals an important truth: what we *feel* behind what we hear matters more than the literal meaning of the words. If someone tells you "I love you" with a flat voice, arms crossed, and eyes glazed over, the words lose their meaning. But when someone looks into your eyes with warmth and presence and simply says "I see you," the impact can be deeper than a thousand love letters.

This is why communication in relationships often goes wrong not because of what's said, but because of what's not aligned. You can have perfect grammar and still break someone's heart. You can use all the right therapeutic vocabulary and still trigger defensiveness. You can rehearse your lines, write the perfect message, explain everything clearly—and still leave the other person confused, disconnected, or hurt. Why? Because if your emotional state is anxious, resentful, withdrawn, or guarded, that energy will always speak louder than your words.

To truly understand this, we need to stop looking at communication as a skill and begin to see it as a field of shared presence. Every time you engage with another human being— especially someone close to you—you are not merely exchanging information. You are co-regulating nervous systems. You are offering or withdrawing safety. You are amplifying or diffusing emotion. You are, whether you realize it or not, engaged in a subtle, continuous feedback loop of emotional signals, which are mostly nonverbal and largely unconscious.

One of the most powerful, yet often invisible, mechanisms in this loop is emotional contagion. This isn't just a poetic concept—it's a neurological reality. Through a set of brain cells called mirror neurons, we are wired to absorb and reflect the emotional states of those around us. When someone in the room is anxious, others tend to become more vigilant. When someone is grounded, calm, and emotionally regulated, that calmness can spread. This is not manipulation—it's biology. Emotions are contagious. And the more emotionally attuned you are, the more likely you are to absorb the internal weather of those you're close to.

The trouble arises when we are unaware of this influence. We bring unprocessed anger into a conversation, and it spreads like wildfire, even if our words sound neutral. We carry tension in our body, and the other person tightens without knowing why. We offer kindness with our lips but impatience with our posture, and the message is scrambled. Then we wonder why things go sideways, why we feel misunderstood, or why conflict escalates so fast.

Awareness is the antidote. When you become responsible not just for your words, but for your *state*, everything changes. This means slowing down before entering a difficult conversation. It means noticing your breathing, your body, your tone. It means asking yourself, "What energy am I bringing into this space?" Because the truth is, how you feel *before* you speak determines how your message lands.

And this leads us to one of the most overlooked superpowers in relational communication: presence.

Presence is not the same as physical proximity. You can be in the same room and still be emotionally absent. You can respond to every text and still be unreachable. True presence is the quality of your attention. It is the depth of your listening. It is what happens when you stop preparing your response and start opening to the other person's experience—without fixing, defending, or interrupting. It is the subtle, sacred gesture of saying, "I'm here. I'm with you. I'm listening not just to your words, but to your heart."

Presence is powerful because it communicates safety. And safety is the prerequisite for vulnerability. When someone feels you are truly present, their nervous system relaxes. Their defenses lower. Their truth becomes more accessible. They feel seen—not as a problem to solve or a story to analyze, but as a human being who matters. You don't need the perfect script to create this effect. You just need your attention, your breath, and your willingness to be with whatever arises.

In this way, presence becomes more than a relational technique—it becomes a form of love. A love that says, "I value you enough to be here now, fully." A love that creates a field where repair is possible, even after rupture. A love that softens hard edges and allows the unspeakable to be spoken without fear.

Of course, none of this means words are unimportant. Language matters. Precision matters. But words are like arrows, and presence is the bow. Without a steady bow, the best arrows miss the mark. Without alignment between tone, body, and intention, communication falters—no matter how wise or practiced your language may be.

This is especially true in moments of high emotion. When you're triggered, flooded, or emotionally raw, your ability to choose your words wisely is compromised. Your tone sharpens. Your posture shifts. Your presence contracts. These moments are when the unconscious parts of communication take over—and if you're not aware of them, they can hijack the conversation.

That's why regulating your state *before* you speak is often more important than rehearsing what to say. You might be right in content, but wrong in energy. And the other person will feel the misalignment. They may not be able to name it, but they will sense it. Their body will tense. Their trust will falter. Their openness will recede.

This is not about perfection. You will miscommunicate. You will be misread. You will have days when your tone betrays your intention, when your words fall flat, when your presence is fractured. That's part of being human. What matters is the willingness to repair—to come back, clarify, and recommit to the connection.

What also matters is listening—not just with your ears, but with your entire being. Listening for the emotion behind the words.

Listening for what's *not* being said. Listening without interrupting the silence, and without jumping ahead in your mind. In this space, connection deepens. Understanding expands. And hearts open—not because everything is resolved, but because everything is welcome.

Real communication is not about perfect clarity. It's about mutual willingness. A willingness to be misunderstood and still stay. A willingness to hear something hard and not collapse. A willingness to say, "This is how I feel," and to trust that the relationship can hold it.

When all the layers of communication—tone, posture, energy, and language—begin to harmonize, something beautiful happens. Conversations become less about managing outcomes and more about being real. You stop rehearsing. You start revealing. You stop performing. You start connecting. And from that connection, relationships become not just functional, but alive.

In the end, the language of the heart is not fluent in syllables alone. It speaks through presence, through resonance, through the courage to be seen and to see. And when you begin to live from this place, you'll find that the words themselves matter less—because the truth you're carrying will already be felt.

You won't just be heard. You'll be received.

5.2 Listening as a Sacred Act

Most of us think we're good listeners. We nod, we wait for our turn, we offer solutions, we say things like "I hear you" and "that must be hard." But truly listening—deeply, actively, sacredly listening—is one of the rarest and most profound gifts we can offer another person. It's not passive, and it's certainly not about waiting for your turn to speak. It's a form of relational devotion, an act of presence so complete that the other person begins to feel not just heard, but *felt*—as if their emotional world is safe in your hands, if only for a moment.

This kind of listening doesn't begin with technique. It begins with intention. The intention to meet another person where they are, without rushing to move them somewhere else. It's easy to hear words, but it's harder—and more important—to hear what lives beneath them. Because people don't always say what they mean. Hurt shows up as sarcasm. Fear as anger. Vulnerability as control. When someone complains about their day, they may be asking for comfort. When they criticize, they may be aching to feel valued. When they ramble, they may be trying to make sense of their pain out loud. To listen with the heart means hearing not just the sentence, but the soul behind it.

This requires slowing down. It requires pausing your inner dialogue—the one that's preparing your response, analyzing what you agree or disagree with, or trying to craft a solution—and instead turning your full attention outward. Listening beyond the story means making contact with the emotional current beneath the words. It means tuning into the person's energy, breath, tone, and body. It's asking yourself, not "What should I say next?" but "What is this person *really* trying to say, and what do they need from me right now?"

The answer is often simpler than we think. Most people don't want advice. They don't want fixes. They want to feel seen. They want to feel like their experience matters. When we jump too quickly to solve or soothe, we unintentionally communicate that the other person's feelings are problems to be erased rather than realities to be honored. And so, while our words may come from care, they land as dismissal.

To truly listen is to trust the other person's capacity. To believe that they are not broken. That they don't need to be rescued. That your job is not to take their pain away, but to help them feel less alone in it. This is empathic resonance. It's the ability to feel *with* someone—not to feel *for* them in a way that consumes you, and not to step *into* their pain as if it's your responsibility to carry it. But to be *beside* them. Attuned. Present. Available. Without drowning.

This is where many sensitive, empathic people struggle. They care so much that they forget where they end and the other person begins. They absorb emotional pain as if it's contagious, and over time, this can lead to emotional burnout or blurred boundaries. True empathic listening doesn't require self-sacrifice. It requires groundedness. The ability to anchor in your own body and presence while opening your heart to someone else. It's a both/and: *I feel you, and I stay with me.*

One of the most powerful ways to offer this kind of listening is through reflection. Reflective listening is not parroting someone's words back to them. It's the art of holding up a mirror, gently and respectfully, so that the person speaking can see themselves more clearly. It's saying things like, "It sounds like you felt really alone in that moment," or "I hear that you're torn between what you want and what you feel responsible for." These reflections don't fix anything. They don't change the person's mind. But they *do* help them feel heard on a deeper level.

When someone feels truly understood, their nervous system relaxes. Defenses soften. Insight emerges. And often, solutions that seemed unreachable become visible—not because you pointed them out, but because the person finally had space to access their own wisdom. Reflective listening is not about guiding someone to your conclusions. It's about helping them listen to themselves more deeply in your presence.

There's a crucial distinction here. Reflection is not correction. It's not interrogation. It's not redirecting the conversation to your own experience. And it's never a subtle form of control. The moment your reflection becomes about influencing the outcome, you're no longer listening—you're steering. Sacred listening is an invitation, not a manipulation.

It also doesn't mean you abandon your own truth. You can deeply listen and still disagree. You can hold someone's pain without validating every belief they hold. The point is not to endorse everything that's said. It's to offer a presence so respectful and accepting that the other person feels safe enough to explore what's *real* for them—without shame, without interruption, without pressure to be anyone but who they are in that moment.

This is how intimacy is built—not through perfect dialogue, but through trust. The trust that you won't turn away when things get messy. That you won't rush to a conclusion just to feel more comfortable. That you are willing to sit with the discomfort of not knowing, not solving, not being right. Just being *with*.

Listening as a sacred act requires nothing more—and nothing less—than your full presence. In a world where people are often reduced to roles, tasks, or social media snapshots, being truly listened to is revolutionary. It reminds people that they are more than their productivity, their mistakes, or their defenses. It reminds them that their inner world matters.

And in the end, listening this way does more than support the other person—it changes *you*. It hones your patience. Deepens your empathy. Strengthens your emotional awareness. You become less reactive. More attuned. More willing to see people as they are, rather than as you wish them to be. And from that place, love becomes something richer. Something quieter. Something real.

5.3 Speaking Your Truth with Love

There is no intimacy without truth. And yet, many of us swallow our truths daily in the name of harmony, acceptance, or safety. We silence our needs because we fear being labeled needy. We edit our feelings so we won't appear dramatic. We avoid conflict by pretending we're fine when we're anything but. Over time, this erodes not only our relationships but our own sense of integrity. We become strangers to ourselves. And the connection we crave begins to feel impossible—not because others have rejected us, but because we never let them meet who we truly are.

Speaking your truth with love is one of the most courageous acts in any relationship. It requires more than honesty. It requires vulnerability. The willingness to be seen not just in your strengths, but in your longings, your fears, your disappointments. The willingness to say, "This matters to me," without knowing how it will be received. The willingness to risk rupture for the sake of realness.

This kind of communication is not about venting. It's not about unloading your emotions on someone else or demanding that they change. It's about sharing your experience in a way that honors both your truth and the dignity of the person receiving it. This is where non-violent communication becomes a powerful guide— not as a formula to follow, but as a mindset to embody.

At its heart, non-violent communication is about translating judgments and demands into observations, feelings, needs, and requests. Instead of saying, "You never listen to me," you might say, "When I'm interrupted, I feel dismissed because I need to feel heard. Can we slow down and try again?" This isn't about being politically correct. It's about being relationally conscious. It's about expressing yourself in a way that's more likely to be heard, less likely to trigger defensiveness, and more anchored in your own emotional truth.

This requires emotional literacy. You need to know what you're feeling before you can express it clearly. You need to understand the need underneath the emotion. Are you angry because your boundary was crossed? Are you sad because you feel disconnected? Are you anxious because something feels unpredictable? The clearer you are with yourself, the clearer you can be with others. And the more likely your message will come from connection rather than reactivity.

Timing matters too. There are moments when the truth is ready to be spoken—but the listener is not ready to receive it. Bringing up something vulnerable when someone is tired, distracted, or emotionally flooded can backfire. The truth deserves a space that can hold it. That means choosing moments of openness, not urgency. It means asking, "Is now a good time for a deeper conversation?" rather than ambushing someone emotionally. It means reading the room—not to avoid speaking, but to protect the *possibility* of being heard.

Equally important is how you *end* the conversation. When truth is shared with love, it doesn't conclude in accusation or demand. It ends with invitation. With curiosity. With openness to dialogue. "Here's what I feel. What's it like for you?" "This is what I need—how do you feel about that?" Speaking your truth with love creates space, not closure. It's a beginning, not a verdict.

And yet, this process is not without risk. You might be misunderstood. You might not get what you ask for. You might speak with care and still be met with defensiveness or withdrawal. That's part of the terrain. Vulnerability doesn't guarantee comfort. But it does guarantee clarity. And with clarity comes freedom. You are no longer hiding. No longer performing. No longer contorting yourself to fit inside someone else's comfort zone. You are choosing to live in alignment, even when that alignment is messy or inconvenient.

This kind of communication, when practiced consistently, transforms relationships. It builds trust—not because things always go smoothly, but because there's a shared commitment to truth. To growth. To meeting each other again and again at the edge of what's real.

And most importantly, speaking your truth with love transforms you. It reclaims your voice. It strengthens your self-respect. It lets the people in your life know that you value connection too much to let it be built on silence or pretense.

In the end, every honest sentence you speak, every feeling you name, every boundary you draw with kindness, becomes a thread in the tapestry of relational integrity. You are weaving something durable. Something warm. Something true.

And perhaps, most sacred of all, you're letting yourself be seen— not as perfect, but as whole. Not as invulnerable, but as real. And that, in the language of the heart, is how love begins. Again and again. Word by word. Truth by truth. Breath by breath.

Chapter 6: The Alchemy of Conflict – Transforming Friction into Deeper Intimacy

Couples often believe that fighting is a sign of dysfunction. They imagine a "healthy" relationship as one free from disagreement, where everything flows with ease and both people remain in harmony at all times. The absence of conflict becomes the benchmark for success, the goal to strive toward. But this belief is not only unrealistic—it's deeply misleading. Relationships without conflict are not necessarily healthy. They are often silent, avoidant, emotionally starved, and saturated with unspoken resentment. True intimacy is not the absence of friction, but the capacity to move through it with honesty, courage, and care.

Conflict is not the enemy of love. It is, paradoxically, one of its most potent teachers. When approached with consciousness, it becomes medicine. It reveals where something is out of alignment—either within one person or between both. It exposes what has been unspoken, what has been unmet, what has been misunderstood. It holds up a mirror to our deepest fears, needs, and beliefs—not to harm us, but to awaken us. In this way, conflict is not a threat to connection; it is the path to deeper connection. It is the fire through which love can be purified, refined, and made real.

This is what most people don't understand. They fear conflict because they've only known it as destructive: yelling, withdrawal, blame, silence. Or they've seen it escalate into rupture, abandonment, or emotional harm. But the problem is not conflict itself—it's the lack of skill, safety, and understanding in how we navigate it. Just as a blade can harm or heal depending on how it's used, so too can conflict either damage or deepen a relationship depending on how it's held.

The first step in this alchemical process is reframing conflict. Rather than seeing it as something to avoid or win, we must learn to see it as a signpost—an indicator that something is asking to be seen more clearly. This might be an unmet need, a personal boundary, a hidden fear, a value misalignment, or a deeper longing for connection. Conflict is not random. It arises when the unconscious meets the conscious, when old patterns bump against present desires, when two truths try to coexist in the same space. It is an invitation—not a punishment.

Disagreement, when honored, becomes a growth edge. It pushes each person to expand their emotional range, deepen their empathy, and articulate their truth more clearly. It asks us to move beyond the familiar roles we've played—pleaser, fixer, controller, avoider—and meet each other from a more grounded, vulnerable place. It challenges our ego and forces us to confront the parts of ourselves we often avoid: our need to be right, our fear of rejection, our discomfort with uncertainty. These are the growing pains of intimacy—not signs that something is broken, but signs that something real is trying to be born.

Of course, not all conflict looks like shouting or raised voices. Often, it's much subtler: sarcasm, emotional distance, passive-aggressive remarks, shutdowns. These forms of tension are no less potent. In fact, they can be more dangerous because they mask the conflict under a veneer of normalcy, making it harder to address. But underneath every argument—whether loud or quiet, dramatic or restrained—lies the same thing: a need trying to be heard.

When someone says, "You never listen to me," they may be expressing a need for presence, for attention, for emotional resonance. When someone accuses their partner of being selfish, they may be yearning for partnership, for shared responsibility, for inclusion. These surface-level criticisms are often clumsy expressions of deeper, more vulnerable truths. But because they're wrapped in judgment or accusation, they trigger defensiveness instead of empathy. And the deeper message gets lost in translation.

The work, then, is to learn how to listen beneath the content. To hear not just what is being said, but what is *really* being communicated. This requires slowing down. It requires curiosity. It requires the willingness to ask, "What is this conflict trying to show us? What need is hiding underneath this complaint? What pain is this anger protecting?" When both people in a relationship begin to ask these questions, something transformative happens. The conflict becomes less about who's right and more about what's real.

This shift doesn't come easily. We are conditioned to defend ourselves. The moment we feel accused, our nervous system reacts. We brace. We prepare our rebuttal. We raise our voice, or we shut down completely. Conflict triggers our survival mechanisms. That's why one of the most powerful skills in relational repair is the ability to stay regulated. To breathe through the discomfort. To notice when you're no longer present. To recognize when your body is preparing for battle rather than connection.

This isn't about suppressing your feelings. It's about staying emotionally anchored so you can express them in a way that creates clarity rather than chaos. The goal is not to erase conflict—it's to change how we hold it. To turn it from a battleground into a bridge. From something we fear into something we can use.

There's a paradox here that many people miss: couples who fight well—who are able to navigate conflict with honesty, accountability, and compassion—are often far more connected than those who rarely argue. This is the intimacy paradox of fighting. Working through a difficult moment together builds trust. It says, "We can face hard things. We can disagree without disconnecting. We can tell the truth without losing each other." That kind of trust cannot be faked. It is earned, moment by moment, in the fire of rupture and repair.

This doesn't mean every conflict needs to end in perfect understanding. Some conflicts remain unresolved, and that's okay. What matters is how they're held. Can both people stay open to learning? Can they validate each other's experience even if they disagree with the perspective? Can they come back to connection, even if the content is still tender?

What often surprises people is that the most meaningful moments in a relationship aren't the easy ones. They're the ones where two people chose to stay—when it would have been easier to leave, shut down, or pretend. They're the moments where truth was spoken, tears were shed, and something deeper was touched. Where one person said, "I didn't realize that hurt you so much," and the other said, "Thank you for listening." These are the moments that bind us—not in fantasy, but in reality. Not in perfection, but in presence.

Of course, not all conflict is healthy. Some dynamics are abusive, coercive, or emotionally unsafe. The ability to alchemize conflict depends on both people being willing to engage with respect, accountability, and care. This work is not about tolerating harm. It's about creating a container where both people can bring their full selves into the light—messy, flawed, and still worthy of love.

When conflict becomes medicine, relationships become laboratories for transformation. You begin to welcome the discomfort, not because it's pleasant, but because it's honest. You stop fearing rupture because you trust in repair. You stop needing peace at any cost because you value truth more than performance. And in that shift, love becomes less about compatibility and more about collaboration—less about finding someone who never hurts you, and more about choosing someone willing to heal with you.

This is not an ideal to strive for. It is a practice. A daily willingness to listen, to name, to soften, to stretch. To meet the hard moments not as enemies, but as teachers. To remember that the person across from you is not the problem—they are your partner. The conflict is not a sign of failure—it is a sign that something in the relationship is evolving, asking to be acknowledged, honored, and reimagined.

So the next time tension arises, try this: pause. Breathe. Ask what truth is trying to come to the surface. Ask what need is trying to be seen. Ask whether this moment—uncomfortable as it may be—is offering an opportunity to come closer, rather than further apart.

Because conflict, when held with presence and intention, is not the end of connection. It's the beginning of something deeper. Something more honest. Something real. It is the forge where trust is strengthened, intimacy is tested, and love is made resilient. And it's in this fire—not in the absence of it—that the most enduring relationships are born.

6.2 The Nervous System During Conflict

Conflict is not just an intellectual disagreement. It is a full-body experience. While words are exchanged and ideas are debated, the nervous system is often waging a war of its own beneath the surface. Understanding this physiological reality is crucial for transforming conflict into connection. Without awareness of the body's role, we risk trying to solve relational problems from a place of emotional dysregulation—where defensiveness, blame, and survival instincts override logic, empathy, and love.

When we enter conflict, our nervous system assesses the situation in milliseconds. It asks: Am I safe? Can I trust this person right now? Are they friend or threat? This primal evaluation happens far faster than conscious reasoning. If our nervous system perceives danger—through a harsh tone, a furrowed brow, or even the memory of a previous argument—it activates what's known as the stress response. This response floods the body with adrenaline and cortisol, preparing us to fight, flee, freeze, or fawn. The heart rate increases. Muscles tense. Breath becomes shallow. Blood rushes away from the prefrontal cortex, the part of the brain responsible for executive functioning, and toward the limbic system, which governs survival. In this state, thoughtful communication becomes nearly impossible.

We all have personal triggers—specific words, expressions, gestures, or tones of voice that act like tripwires. These triggers are often rooted in past experiences, especially from early childhood or formative relationships. For some, being interrupted may evoke memories of never being heard. For others, a partner walking away during a disagreement might feel like abandonment. These reactions are rarely about the present alone. They are echoes from the past, reactivated in real-time by the nervous system's need to protect us from perceived threat.

Becoming aware of these triggers is not about assigning blame—it's about owning our patterns. When we can name what activates us, we reclaim a measure of power over it. We can begin to communicate these patterns to our partners, not as accusations, but as insights. For example: "When I hear a sharp tone, I notice I get defensive because it reminds me of being criticized growing up." This kind of self-awareness helps de-escalate tension. It shifts the conversation from attack-and-defend to understand-and-support. It also allows our partners to engage with greater compassion, rather than accidentally triggering old wounds without context.

Even with self-awareness, however, the body sometimes overrides intention. Once the stress response has been activated, it takes time for the body and brain to return to baseline. This is where the "20-minute rule" comes in. Neuroscience shows that after a spike in stress hormones, it typically takes the body about twenty minutes to metabolize those chemicals and begin calming down. During this window, even the best communication tools can fail, simply because the rational mind is offline. Continuing the conversation in this state often leads to more misunderstanding and pain.

This is why taking a break is not avoidance—it's wisdom. But the way we take a break matters. Simply walking out or shutting down can feel like rejection to the other person, triggering their own nervous system response. Instead, it's essential to communicate clearly: "I'm feeling overwhelmed and I know I can't speak clearly right now. I need twenty minutes to regulate myself, and then I want to come back and talk this through." When done with intention and transparency, this kind of pause preserves connection rather than damaging it. It gives both people a chance to return to the conversation with more presence and less reactivity.

Regulating the nervous system is not only a solo process. In relationships, we are constantly co-regulating. This means our emotional states influence each other in real-time. A calm voice can soothe a racing heart. A reassuring glance can ease tension. Gentle touch, steady breathing, soft eye contact—these are not just gestures of affection, but physiological signals of safety. When one partner is able to stay anchored during conflict, they can become a stabilizing presence, helping the other person return to equilibrium. This is not about taking responsibility for the other's emotions. It's about offering a safe space for regulation to occur naturally through presence.

This is especially powerful when both people are aware of their nervous systems and committed to co-regulation. Instead of escalating each other's defenses, they become partners in creating calm. They notice when one starts to dysregulate and suggest a breath, a break, a change of tone. They speak not just with their words, but with their nervous systems. They know that every argument is not just a conversation—it's a biological event. And they treat it with the care and slowness that such an event deserves.

In some relationships, the nervous system has been so chronically activated that even small disagreements feel like threats. This is often the case when past trauma has not been addressed. In these situations, conflict becomes a reenactment of old pain, and the body prepares for war even when the topic is benign. Healing in this context requires more than communication tools. It requires nervous system healing: through therapy, somatic practices, breathwork, and a consistent experience of relational safety over time.

Ultimately, learning to regulate during conflict is a practice of relational maturity. It means taking responsibility not just for your words, but for the state from which you speak. It means learning to listen to your body, to pause when needed, to come back to the conversation when you are able to truly engage. And it means co-creating a space where both people can remain human, flawed, and triggered—and still be safe, still be loved, still be reachable.

6.3 Tools for Conscious Conflict Resolution

Once we understand how conflict affects the nervous system, we are better equipped to respond rather than react. But understanding alone isn't enough. We need practices—repeatable, embodied frameworks that help us move through disagreements with clarity, compassion, and care. Conscious conflict resolution is not about avoiding friction. It's about facing it with skill. It is the art of staying connected while navigating discomfort. Of standing in your truth without making the other wrong. Of transforming rupture into repair, and resistance into deeper understanding.

At the heart of this process lies a simple but powerful sequence: pause, breathe, respond. It sounds elementary, but its effects are profound. The pause creates a moment of space between stimulus and reaction. It allows the automatic response—the snarky comment, the defensive jab, the passive-aggressive withdrawal—to dissolve before it takes form. The breath activates the parasympathetic nervous system, sending a signal to the body that it is safe to stay. And the response, now freed from reactivity, can be shaped with intention. It can express truth without blame. It can ask for change without shaming. It can hold difference without collapse.

This pause-breathe-respond rhythm is not a trick. It is a practice of presence. It requires you to stay inside your own experience, to resist the urge to fix or punish, and to become curious about what is really happening—both in you and in the other. And from that curiosity, resolution becomes possible.

One of the keys to this kind of resolution is the ability to separate the person from the behavior. This distinction can shift the entire emotional tone of a conflict. When we collapse the two—when we say "You're selfish" instead of "That action felt inconsiderate"—we turn a behavior into a character judgment. This instantly puts the other person on the defensive. But when we stay with the specific action, we leave space for accountability without humiliation. We say, "I care about you, and I want to address something that didn't feel good," rather than "There's something wrong with who you are."

Maintaining this distinction requires emotional discipline. It asks us to speak from our experience rather than our projections. To say, "I felt hurt when that happened," rather than, "You always hurt me." It keeps the focus on impact rather than intent, on present behavior rather than past baggage. This doesn't mean avoiding hard truths. It means delivering them with respect. With care. With the understanding that love doesn't mean always agreeing—but it *does* mean always honoring each other's humanity.

From this foundation, we can begin to move toward solutions. But here, too, the goal is not compromise for its own sake. Many people equate conflict resolution with finding the middle ground—each person gives something up to preserve the peace. But there is another path: the win-win-win. This is the solution that honors not only your needs and your partner's needs, but also the needs of the relationship itself.

This requires creativity. It asks both people to move beyond positions and into values. Instead of debating over *what* should happen, they explore *why* it matters. For instance, if one person wants more space and the other wants more closeness, a win-win-

win doesn't ask either to sacrifice—it asks them to co-create a rhythm where space and closeness can both exist in a way that feels good to both. This might mean shared time is more intentional and solo time is more respected. The point is not to split the difference, but to honor the essence of what each person needs.

The relationship itself is the third entity in this equation. It has its own needs: trust, safety, shared purpose, connection. When we center this third entity, we stop trying to "win" the argument. We start asking, "What does the relationship need to thrive?" Sometimes, this means letting go of being right. Sometimes it means naming a difficult truth. But always, it means orienting toward connection rather than control.

All of this takes practice. It takes mistakes, and repair, and more mistakes. But with each attempt, the muscle of conscious conflict resolution grows stronger. The conversations get deeper. The ruptures heal faster. The relationship becomes less brittle and more alive.

You start to trust not that everything will always be easy—but that when it's hard, you'll find your way through. Together. With breath. With truth. With love.

And that is what transforms conflict into alchemy. Not the absence of pain, but the presence of commitment. Not perfect behavior, but the willingness to keep returning—to yourself, to each other, to the table where love is built not in spite of conflict, but through it.

Chapter 7: The Wounds That Bind –
Healing Trauma's Impact on Love

"Trauma is not what happens to you, but what happens inside you as a result of what happened to you." – Gabor Maté

7.1 Understanding Relational Trauma

No matter how skillful we become in communication or how present we try to be in conflict, some invisible threads still pull us back into old patterns—patterns that confuse us, sabotage intimacy, or leave us feeling helpless, unseen, or unworthy of love. These threads are not merely habits or quirks. They are wounds. More specifically, they are the imprints of relational trauma: the internalized impact of moments when connection was broken, safety was compromised, or the fundamental experience of being valued and protected was absent. And unless we learn to see these wounds for what they are—not as flaws, but as adaptations—we remain bound by them. They will shape who we choose, how we relate, what we fear, and how close we dare to get.

Relational trauma is not always obvious. When we hear the word "trauma," we often imagine war zones, car accidents, abuse. These are what psychologists call "Big T" traumas—catastrophic events that overwhelm the nervous system and create clear psychological disruption. But many of the wounds that affect our ability to love and be loved come not from what was done to us, but from what was missing. They stem from repeated experiences of neglect, dismissal, or emotional misattunement. They're what we might call "little t" traumas: subtle, chronic ruptures in care that accumulate over time and leave deep, invisible marks.

The child who was always told to be quiet when upset. The teenager whose vulnerability was met with ridicule. The partner whose boundaries were never respected. These are not headline traumas—but they are the kind that shape our capacity for intimacy in adulthood. They teach us that it's not safe to be fully seen. That love must be earned through compliance or perfection. That our needs are too much. Or that closeness will inevitably lead to abandonment. These beliefs, even if unspoken, form the core of our relational blueprint. And until they are examined and healed, they govern our relationships like an unseen script.

Trauma is not the event—it is the adaptation. It is the way the body, mind, and heart learn to survive in the face of repeated pain. For some, this means shutting down completely—numbing emotions, avoiding closeness, or building a fortress around the heart. For others, it means over-functioning—people-pleasing, caretaking, or anxiously monitoring the emotional weather of everyone around them in a desperate attempt to feel safe. Neither of these responses are wrong. They are ingenious strategies developed in the absence of secure attachment. But what protects us in childhood can imprison us in adulthood.

One of the most common ways unhealed trauma shows up in love is through what's known as trauma bonding. This is not intimacy—it's entanglement. It occurs when two people connect through shared pain, rather than shared values or mutual respect. The bond feels intense, magnetic, and even euphoric at times, but it's fueled by reactivity, not stability. One partner's abandonment wound triggers the other's fear of engulfment. One person's volatility soothes the other's need for chaos. The dynamic may mimic passion, but beneath it lies repetition—not revelation. Trauma bonds are cyclical, built on highs and lows, fueled by chemistry that often has more to do with familiarity than compatibility.

In contrast, healthy attachment grows slowly, grounded in safety, consistency, and the mutual honoring of boundaries and truth. It doesn't always feel as exhilarating at first, especially for those used to emotional rollercoasters. It feels calmer, more boring even—but only to a nervous system accustomed to chaos. Over time, though, it's this calmness that creates the space for true depth, playfulness, and emotional intimacy. Healthy love doesn't keep you guessing. It doesn't spike your adrenaline. It doesn't require you to abandon yourself to be chosen. It invites you to come home—to yourself and to another, simultaneously.

But for many trauma survivors, healthy love can feel threatening. The nervous system, primed for danger, can interpret calm as suspicious. A partner who respects your space may be misread as distant. A disagreement without yelling may feel like disconnection. The body has learned to equate intensity with intimacy, drama with aliveness, and pain with presence. And so, even when we consciously want safety, we unconsciously recreate danger. We sabotage or push away relationships that don't match our internal template, not because we don't want love, but because we don't yet recognize it when it arrives.

This is where the inner work begins—not with blaming ourselves for our patterns, but with honoring the intelligence behind them. Every maladaptive behavior is an echo of something that made sense once. People-pleasing may have once ensured safety in a volatile home. Emotional withdrawal may have once protected against overwhelming shame. Hypervigilance may have once been necessary for survival. To change these behaviors, we must first understand their origin—and thank them for getting us this far.

One particularly misunderstood trauma response is the fawn response, often overshadowed by the more well-known fight, flight, and freeze. Fawning is the reflexive urge to appease, accommodate, or please others at the expense of one's own needs, boundaries, or authenticity. It is common among those who experienced emotional neglect, chronic criticism, or unpredictable caregiving. The child who learned to stay invisible to avoid punishment becomes the adult who says "yes" when they mean "no," who anticipates everyone else's needs before their own, and who finds validation in being useful rather than being themselves.

Fawning may look like kindness, generosity, or flexibility—but it is not born of abundance. It is a trauma strategy. It keeps the peace by erasing the self. And while it may earn temporary approval, it creates deep internal resentment. Over time, the fawn response leads to burnout, loss of identity, and relational dynamics where one person gives and the other takes, often without even realizing it. Healing from fawning involves reclaiming one's voice, learning to tolerate disapproval, and building the internal safety necessary to risk being authentic, even when it might disappoint others.

Healing relational trauma is not about becoming perfect. It is not about arriving at a place where triggers never happen or old wounds never resurface. It is about developing the capacity to respond differently—to pause, to reflect, to choose a new way. It is about creating relationships where repair is possible, where ruptures are met with humility rather than shame, and where the goal is not to avoid pain but to be present with it until it transforms.

This healing does not happen in isolation. While trauma often originates in relationship, it must also be healed in relationship. Safe, attuned connection is the medicine. Whether through therapy, partnership, community, or friendship, the nervous system learns new truths not through logic, but through lived experience. When someone sees you in your pain and doesn't turn away, the body begins to relax. When you set a boundary and the world doesn't collapse, trust begins to grow. When you stay, when you speak, when you risk, and something better happens—healing begins.

But this healing also requires solitude. The work of noticing your own patterns, grieving your own losses, and learning to soothe your own pain cannot be outsourced. It is in the quiet moments— when you choose to sit with discomfort instead of escaping it, when you tell yourself the truth instead of performing a role, when you forgive yourself for the choices you made in survival mode—that real integration occurs.

Over time, the past begins to loosen its grip. The same triggers no longer hijack your reactions. The same fears no longer dictate your choices. The same wounds still exist—but they are no longer in the driver's seat. You start to love from a place of wholeness, rather than hunger. You start to see conflict not as abandonment, but as information. You start to choose relationships not from desperation, but from discernment. And most importantly, you start to relate to yourself not as broken, but as someone who adapted brilliantly—and who is now ready to grow beyond the adaptation.

This is the path of relational healing. It is not linear. It is not always graceful. But it is deeply human. And at every step, it asks not for perfection, but for presence. For honesty. For the willingness to try again.

Because even the deepest wounds can become portals to the most profound love—not despite the pain, but because of how it shaped your capacity to feel, to care, and to choose differently. Not all that binds us is beautiful. But all that binds us can be made into something beautiful—if we are willing to look, to feel, and to heal. Together.

7.2 The Body Remembers What the Mind Forgets

Long after the conscious mind has filed away events into the archive of the past, the body still keeps the score. While we might not remember the exact moment a parent dismissed our emotions, or the specific tone used by a partner that made us feel small, our nervous system does. It remembers through shallow breath, tight shoulders, clenched jaws, restless sleep, and that sudden need to flee a conversation we logically know is safe. Trauma is not just a memory; it's a physiological imprint. And in relationships, this imprint becomes a script we don't even realize we're following.

Understanding trauma purely through narrative—by recounting what happened—is only one dimension of healing. For many, the trauma isn't in what they remember, but in what they cannot recall clearly, yet still feel viscerally. A partner raises their voice slightly, and the stomach drops. Someone turns away during an argument, and the chest tightens, as if suffocated. These reactions are not simply emotional. They are somatic. The body has learned to associate certain signals with danger, even when the present moment offers no real threat.

This is why somatic awareness is vital in relational healing. It teaches us to listen to the body's language: the sudden heat in the cheeks, the heaviness in the limbs, the buzzing in the fingers, the urge to run or to disappear. These are messages, not malfunctions. When we become attuned to these sensations, we begin to map how our history inhabits our present. We realize that we may be responding to our partner's current tone, but with the intensity of a parent's past cruelty. We may be reacting to a mild disagreement as if it were a threat of abandonment. This is not irrational—it is the body's attempt to protect us from what it believes is a repetition of old pain.

In relationships, this body-based imprint of trauma can manifest in many ways. One of the most common is hypervigilance: a state of constant scanning for emotional danger. The hypervigilant nervous system doesn't rest. It watches for subtle changes in tone, word choice, and facial expression. It assumes the worst and prepares for it. A delayed text becomes a sign of disinterest. A tired sigh sounds like rejection. Silence feels like betrayal. And all of this happens before conscious thought can intervene.

Hypervigilance is exhausting—not just for the person experiencing it, but also for their partner. It creates a relational field of tension, where trust is fragile and the smallest rupture can feel catastrophic. The person in hypervigilance may crave connection desperately, but their body is on high alert, unable to relax into the very closeness they long for. It's like trying to sleep with one eye open—never fully resting, never fully receiving.

On the other end of the spectrum lies dissociation, another somatic survival strategy. Where hypervigilance keeps the system alert, dissociation numbs it. In moments of emotional intensity, someone who dissociates may suddenly go blank, zone out, or become emotionally absent. Their words may continue, but their presence vanishes. Dissociation is not a choice—it is a protective mechanism the body employs when it believes full presence would be overwhelming or unsafe. In relationships, this can be confusing and painful. A partner may interpret dissociation as apathy or stonewalling, when in fact it is a sign that the person is overwhelmed and trying to survive.

The challenge with dissociation is that it often goes unnoticed by the person experiencing it. It can feel like fatigue, confusion, or simply "not being there." It can happen during arguments, sex, or even moments of affection. The body exits before the mind can catch up. And because the person doesn't fully register their absence, they can't repair the disconnection afterward.

Learning to return from dissociation begins with anchoring into the body. This might involve noticing the breath, feeling the ground beneath the feet, or even placing a hand over the heart to create a sense of self-contact. These simple gestures can serve as doorways back into the present. For some, this process is slow. It may require external support, such as a therapist or a patient partner who understands that emotional absence is not always a sign of emotional rejection.

What's crucial is that we stop pathologizing these responses. Hypervigilance and dissociation are not flaws. They are brilliant, if outdated, strategies the nervous system developed to protect us. The work is not to eliminate them, but to become aware of them, to appreciate their origins, and to gently guide the body toward new possibilities. This may mean creating rituals of safety before difficult conversations. It may mean establishing agreements around conflict resolution. It may mean learning to ask for space—not from avoidance, but from care.

Somatic awareness also allows us to recognize when others are moving through their trauma responses. Instead of taking it personally when a partner shuts down or becomes anxious, we learn to ask deeper questions. We see the nervous system in action and respond not with reactivity, but with compassion. This doesn't mean excusing harmful behavior. It means contextualizing it. It means holding both people's histories as part of the relational dynamic, without allowing them to dominate it.

In truth, the body is not our enemy—it is our most honest ally. It tells the truth even when our minds have learned to lie. And when we learn to speak its language, we can stop reenacting the past and begin rewriting our future.

7.3 Post-Traumatic Growth in Relationships

Though trauma leaves deep imprints on our ability to love and be loved, it does not have to define us. In fact, one of the most profound paradoxes of healing is that moving through trauma can actually increase our capacity for connection. When we face our pain, when we meet our wounded parts with care rather than shame, something extraordinary happens. We become more compassionate, more attuned, more available—not despite what we've endured, but because of how we've transformed it.

This is the essence of post-traumatic growth. It is not just recovery. It is expansion. It is the process by which survivors of trauma emerge with a deeper appreciation for life, a greater sense of personal strength, and a renewed ability to connect authentically. In relationships, this growth is especially meaningful. It turns past suffering into relational wisdom. It allows us to love more skillfully, more humbly, and with more awareness.

Many who walk this path embody the archetype of the wounded healer. These are not people who have conquered pain once and for all, but those who have made peace with their story. They don't pretend to have it all together. Instead, they've developed a relationship with their vulnerability—a willingness to share their truth, to offer empathy without losing boundaries, and to hold space for others without collapsing. The wounded healer knows that healing is never complete. It's a lifelong spiral. And in that humility lies great power.

Bringing this awareness into relationships means becoming trauma-informed—not in a clinical sense, but in a human one. It means understanding that everyone carries invisible wounds, and that those wounds shape how we listen, how we argue, how we reach for one another. It means recognizing that behaviors like shutting down, becoming defensive, or needing reassurance are often not immaturity or manipulation, but echoes of old pain. To be trauma-informed is not to excuse all behavior. It is to approach it with curiosity. To ask not, "What's wrong with you?" but, "What happened to you?" and, even more radically, "What is possible now?"

Trauma-informed relationships are not defined by perfect communication. They are defined by repair. They are marked by the ability to notice when old patterns are resurfacing, to name them without blame, and to co-create a different outcome. This requires courage, patience, and above all, consistency. The nervous system doesn't heal through grand gestures. It heals through repeated experiences of safety. It learns to trust not words, but follow-through. Not promises, but patterns.

This is why building safety together is not a one-time event. It is a daily practice. It involves showing up even when it's hard. It involves keeping agreements, being transparent about your internal world, and listening not just to what is said, but to what is felt. It involves learning one another's triggers, not to avoid them forever, but to meet them with skill and compassion. And when ruptures happen—as they inevitably will—it involves returning. Not perfectly. But honestly.

As partners, friends, or family members, we become co-regulators in each other's healing. We offer grounding when the other is spiraling. We speak softly when the world gets loud. We hold each other accountable, not from judgment, but from love. We remind each other that it's okay to be a work in progress. That trust can be rebuilt. That love, when made conscious, can heal what fear once fractured.

Post-traumatic growth also redefines strength. In a culture that often equates strength with stoicism or independence, healing teaches us a different model. Here, strength is vulnerability with boundaries. It's softness that doesn't collapse. It's being able to say, "I'm struggling right now," without losing your center. It's choosing to connect when every cell in your body wants to protect. It's staying when it would be easier to leave—and leaving when staying would mean self-betrayal.

There is a quiet revolution that happens in relationships shaped by this kind of growth. The focus shifts from performance to presence. From roles to reality. From trying to be lovable to realizing we already are. The relationship becomes a space not to escape ourselves, but to come home to ourselves. Not to get what we never had, but to create what we always deserved.

In this space, the past still lives—but it no longer leads. The body still remembers—but now it remembers safety too. And the heart, once armored, learns to open—not because there are no risks, but because love is worth the risk.

This is not the end of the healing journey. It is its beginning. And it's a journey best walked together—with open eyes, open hands, and an open heart.

Chapter 8: The Sacred Masculine and Divine Feminine – Integrating Inner Polarities

"The privilege of a lifetime is being who you are." – Joseph Campbell

8.1 Beyond Gender Roles – Internal Energetic Dynamics

For most of modern history, discussions about masculine and feminine qualities have been entangled with rigid gender roles and societal expectations. Yet beneath the cultural constructs, beyond the binaries of man and woman, lies a deeper truth: we all carry within us a dynamic interplay of energies often described as "masculine" and "feminine"—not as biological imperatives, but as archetypal forces. These energies do not correspond strictly to male or female identities. Rather, they represent complementary principles that govern how we act, feel, lead, listen, create, destroy, protect, and yield.

In the context of relationships, these inner polarities shape not only how we relate to others but also how we relate to ourselves. When one side is underdeveloped or suppressed, we find ourselves acting from imbalance—overcontrolling or overly passive, emotionally distant or emotionally flooded, too rigid or too fluid. True intimacy, not only with another but with life itself, arises when we begin to recognize these inner dynamics, integrate them consciously, and learn to let each come forward with purpose and integrity.

Masculine energy is not about domination, stoicism, or suppression of emotion. That is a cultural distortion—a shadow form. In its essence, the sacred masculine is about direction. It's the internal compass that allows us to move forward with clarity, to create boundaries that protect what matters, and to hold presence in the face of chaos. The healthy masculine is the container: strong, yet not forceful; steady, yet not stagnant. It is the part of us that says, "I will take care of this," not from ego, but from commitment. It is that part of us that steps into the unknown with focus, that organizes our inner and outer world, that says "yes" to purpose even when fear whispers "no."

In contrast, the divine feminine is the flow. It is intuition, emotional sensitivity, creativity, sensuality, and the capacity to surrender into the unfolding of life. She is not weak. She is yielding, which is something altogether different. While the masculine draws the map, the feminine feels the terrain. She listens—not just with ears, but with the body, with the gut, with the heart. She responds to what is, rather than imposing what should be. She dances with chaos instead of trying to control it. And in doing so, she invites others to soften, to open, to feel.

We all carry both of these energies within us. Yet many of us have been conditioned to favor one and distrust the other. In a world that rewards productivity, assertiveness, and mental logic, masculine traits are often overdeveloped at the expense of feminine wisdom. We are taught to act, not to feel. To build, not to receive. To solve, not to sense. As a result, many people—regardless of gender—walk through life disconnected from their own emotional world, suspicious of their inner rhythms, and unable to fully rest into intimacy. Others, conversely, may find themselves overwhelmed by their emotional sensitivity, drowning in empathy without direction or structure, lacking the inner masculine capacity to discern, act, and hold space.

The work, then, is not to choose one over the other, but to integrate. Integration means more than balance. Balance suggests a kind of equal division—half structure, half flow. But life doesn't work that way. Some moments call for more masculine energy—clarity, firmness, boundaries. Others ask for the feminine—softness, receptivity, vulnerability. Integration is the art of listening deeply to what is needed in a given moment and allowing the appropriate energy to step forward.

This internal integration creates external harmony. When we're aligned within, our relationships begin to mirror that. We stop looking for someone to complete us, to carry the qualities we've disowned. The person who once seemed attractive because they "had what we lacked" no longer holds the same power over us. Instead, relationships become a space where integrated beings meet—not to fill voids in each other, but to explore and expand what is already whole.

To access the inner masculine is to cultivate boundaries with compassion. It is to say no without guilt, to act from purpose rather than impulse, to protect your peace without needing permission. It allows you to stay grounded in the face of emotional turbulence—yours or someone else's—and to show up with integrity when you'd rather shut down or avoid. It's the voice inside that says, "You've got this," and the spine that supports that voice when life tests your resolve.

Accessing the inner feminine, on the other hand, is to deepen your relationship with the unseen. It's to feel more than you can explain, to trust the rhythm of things even when logic fails, to allow grief or joy to move through you without censorship. It is the part of you that knows how to listen—to a partner, to your body, to the seasons of your soul. It allows you to receive love without questioning whether you've earned it. And it's the creative force that turns chaos into beauty, silence into song, stillness into growth.

Many relational conflicts are rooted in a disconnection from these inner polarities. When a person suppresses their feminine energy, they may struggle with emotional intimacy, dismiss their intuition, or feel uncomfortable with expressions of vulnerability. Their relationships may feel efficient but cold, structured but starved of depth. Conversely, someone overly identified with the feminine might feel everything intensely but lack the tools to hold themselves through the intensity. They may feel easily overwhelmed, unable to assert their needs, or chronically drawn to partners who "rescue" them—mirroring a missing internal masculine.

When we begin to re-integrate these archetypes within ourselves, something profound happens. Our inner world becomes more fluid, more nuanced, more resilient. We become less reactive, more responsive. We're no longer governed by extremes or trapped in outdated gender scripts. We stop performing roles and start living truths.

This work is especially liberating in the context of healing gendered expectations. Many women, for example, have been conditioned to suppress their assertiveness in the name of being likable or accommodating. Reclaiming the sacred masculine within allows them to access a fierce protectiveness of self, to speak boundaries without apology, to step into leadership without guilt. Likewise, many men have been taught to hide their emotional world, to fear softness as weakness, to equate vulnerability with failure. Reclaiming the divine feminine opens the door to a deeper sense of aliveness, relational presence, and emotional courage.

For those who identify outside the binary, the conversation becomes even richer. Here, integration is not a balancing act between two opposing poles, but a full spectrum of energetic expressions. It's about honoring the complexity of inner dynamics without forcing them into predefined shapes. It's about allowing your internal world to be as diverse, nuanced, and fluid as you are.

Ultimately, integrating the sacred masculine and divine feminine is not about self-improvement—it's about self-remembrance. It's a return to wholeness. A movement away from fragmentation toward integration. When we live from this place, relationships become not just containers for connection but crucibles for transformation. They become the sacred ground where we practice bringing both energies to the table—where we learn when to hold and when to yield, when to speak and when to listen, when to lead and when to follow.

This is not a destination. It's a lifelong unfolding. A daily invitation to tune in, to ask what is needed now, and to trust that you hold within you the capacity to meet life from both power and presence. From clarity and compassion. From the strength of the sacred masculine and the depth of the divine feminine.

Not as a performance. Not as a role. But as who you already are—once you remember.

8.2 Healing Wounded Masculine and Feminine Patterns

We live in a world where masculine and feminine energies have not only been misunderstood but deeply wounded by centuries of cultural conditioning, generational trauma, and systemic imbalance. These wounds are not just abstract notions; they live in our bodies, shape our thoughts, and show up every day in the way we relate to ourselves and others. To begin healing these wounds is to dismantle internalized roles we didn't consciously choose, and to reintroduce ourselves to a more authentic way of being—one that integrates both strength and softness, presence and surrender.

The wounded masculine is often characterized by a fear of vulnerability masked as dominance. It may manifest as aggression, control, emotional suppression, workaholism, or a compulsive need to prove worth through action and achievement. These patterns are not signs of inherent malice but protective adaptations. The man who cannot express tenderness may have been taught that emotions are weaknesses. The person who retreats into work may have grown up equating success with love. Behind the armor of the wounded masculine lies a fragile self-image—one that believes it must perform, conquer, and never falter in order to be respected or loved.

This distortion doesn't only show up in men. Women and non-binary individuals can also embody the wounded masculine. The mother who sacrifices everything and controls every aspect of her home may be running on wounded masculine energy—believing that if she does not hold everything together, she will lose herself or be unloved. The leader who appears invulnerable and dismisses emotional intelligence may simply be defending against the fear that softness equals irrelevance in a world that prizes efficiency over empathy.

The wounded feminine, on the other hand, often reveals itself through patterns of emotional chaos, self-abandonment, codependency, and manipulative behaviors. She may appear as the martyr who gives until she is empty, the seductress who uses charm as currency, or the victim who feels helpless in the face of her own emotional tides. These too are survival strategies. The child who learned that being overly accommodating earned approval might grow into an adult who never says no. The teenager who was punished for expressing anger might learn to express pain indirectly, through silence or guilt. The woman who was sexualized too early may unconsciously use her body as the only source of power she knows.

Like the masculine, wounded feminine energy does not belong exclusively to women. Any person can carry this pattern within them. The person who becomes emotionally flooded and unable to make decisions when stress hits, or the individual who pleads, manipulates, or withdraws to avoid conflict, may be acting from a place of unhealed feminine wounding. It is not about blaming these expressions, but about recognizing them as signs that something deeper within us is asking for integration.

Healing begins with acknowledgment. It requires a kind of inner honesty that is not harsh but courageous. To recognize your wounded masculine might mean seeing how often you interrupt others, dominate conversations, avoid emotional topics, or equate your productivity with your value. To see your wounded feminine might mean noticing how often you people-please, suppress anger, romanticize suffering, or lose yourself in relationships. This is not about self-blame. It is about bringing clarity to what has been unconscious.

As we begin to heal these patterns, what emerges is a more grounded version of our internal energies. The healthy masculine is not performative; it is presence. It holds space without needing to control. It speaks truth without the need to dominate. It acts with clarity, not force. It does not need to be louder than others to feel powerful. Its power lies in its rootedness, its focus, and its integrity.

The healthy feminine, in turn, is not chaotic or helpless. She is wise, intuitive, and embodied. She receives with openness but also knows when to say no. She feels deeply but is not consumed by emotion. She trusts her cycles, honors her desires, and expresses her needs with clarity. She doesn't manipulate to be heard; she speaks with self-respect.

Reclaiming these healthy forms is not about flipping a switch. It is an ongoing process of unlearning and relearning. It might involve developing emotional literacy for the first time, practicing assertiveness, or creating rituals that allow both the masculine and feminine to thrive within you. The dance is subtle. It might mean noticing when you're pushing too hard and choosing to soften. Or realizing when you're deferring your truth and deciding to speak with strength.

When we reclaim our authentic power—by integrating both our internal masculine and feminine—we stop outsourcing our sense of safety, love, or worth to others. We stop expecting our partners to be the protector, the savior, the nurturer, the therapist. Instead, we become fuller, more sovereign individuals capable of meeting others not from lack, but from wholeness.

This integration doesn't mean we never fall into old patterns. It means we recognize them more quickly, recover more gracefully, and relate from a place of growing awareness rather than unconscious repetition. We stop perpetuating the wounds that shaped us, and begin co-creating a new legacy—one where masculine and feminine energies dance in mutual respect and creative tension, rather than in a war for dominance.

8.3 Polarity and Attraction in Relationships

Attraction, when stripped of superficial traits, is energy meeting energy. Chemistry is often described as unexplainable, but at its core lies a potent principle: polarity. When two people embody opposing but complementary energetic states—typically labeled as masculine and feminine—there is a charge, a tension, a pull. It's not about roles or appearances. It's about the dynamic interaction between directive and receptive forces, between structure and spontaneity, between clarity and mystery.

In its highest form, polarity is not a game. It's an invitation. It calls each partner into deeper presence with themselves and each other. The partner embodying more masculine energy holds the space—offers direction, containment, and steadiness. The partner embodying more feminine energy offers flow—emotional expression, sensual presence, and intuitive insight. When this is conscious, it's electric. It nourishes both partners without collapsing either. The masculine is inspired by the feminine's radiance; the feminine feels safe and seen within the masculine's clarity.

Problems arise not from the existence of polarity, but from its distortion or absence. When both partners lean heavily into the same energy, the dynamic can become flat or competitive. Two people both in masculine drive might end up constantly planning, fixing, and organizing—yet emotional intimacy remains elusive. Two partners both in feminine mode might connect deeply on emotion but struggle to move forward in decision-making or direction. Neither is wrong. But without the tension of difference, passion can wane.

Conversely, when polarity is present but unconscious, it often slips into shadow forms. A masculine energy that becomes controlling. A feminine energy that becomes manipulative. These distortions still create charge, but it's the charge of unresolved trauma, not conscious intimacy. The key is to recognize the difference between chemistry rooted in growth and that fueled by wounds.

Maintaining polarity in long-term relationships requires intentionality. Over time, especially in domestic life, partners often become more alike. They share tasks, make joint decisions, adopt similar routines. While this deepens companionship, it can also erode erotic tension. The familiarity that breeds comfort can also breed energetic sameness. To rekindle polarity, partners must consciously step back into differentiated energetic roles—not as fixed identities, but as playful invitations.

This doesn't mean adhering to gender stereotypes. A woman can embody masculine energy during the day—leading a business, setting boundaries, making tough calls—and then consciously relax into her feminine in the evening through dance, stillness, or emotional expression. A man can spend the day in his feminine—creating art, parenting with softness, grieving—and then step into his masculine through action, structure, or decision-making. Polarity is fluid. The dance is dynamic.

It also helps to understand that polarity shifts naturally over time. Life phases, hormonal changes, stress, and inner growth all influence which energy feels most accessible. During crisis or high-stress periods, someone might need to lean into masculine decisiveness. In times of healing or reflection, the feminine might take precedence. The healthiest relationships allow for this ebb and flow without panic. Partners give each other space to shift, adapt, and rediscover themselves without clinging to one "correct" energetic posture.

What matters is not rigid roles, but conscious presence. When both partners are self-aware, they can navigate polarity with creativity. They can ask, "What's needed now?" rather than defaulting to scripts. They can recognize when polarity is slipping into fusion—when both partners start mirroring each other so closely that they lose their own essence. And they can recalibrate—not through blame, but through intention.

This might look like one partner creating a container—a plan, a ritual, a decision—so the other can soften into expression or receptivity. It might mean carving out space for sensuality, play, or silence. It might involve vulnerability—admitting when you're too much in your head or too lost in emotion, and inviting the other to bring their complementary energy forward.

Polarity doesn't mean someone always leads and someone always follows. It means both have access to both energies, and both honor the beauty in each. It's not about power over, but power with. When approached with reverence, polarity becomes a sacred engine—a force that drives connection, intimacy, and shared evolution.

In this space, attraction is no longer a fleeting spark. It becomes a living current. A conversation between archetypes. A dance that is both ancient and new, choreographed not by society's expectations, but by the wisdom of your own energy in dialogue with another's. And when two people meet here—rooted in their essence, fluid in their expression, conscious in their play—they create something far more enduring than chemistry. They create union. Not through sameness, but through the charged beauty of difference.

Chapter 9: The Attachment Revolution – Rewiring Your Love Patterns

Secure attachment can be developed at any age through conscious relationship practices and internal healing work.

9.1 Understanding Your Attachment Style

The roots of how we love are planted long before we even understand the meaning of the word. Our first experiences of safety, nourishment, attention, and distress—most often within the arms of a parent or primary caregiver—set the tone for how we later experience closeness, intimacy, and conflict. These early blueprints become the silent architecture of our emotional lives. They shape how we reach for connection, how we handle space and distance, how we interpret silence or a raised voice, and how we respond when love feels uncertain or threatening.

The concept of attachment is not new. Psychologists have studied it for decades, yet only in recent years has it begun to enter everyday language. We hear people casually refer to themselves as "anxiously attached" or "emotionally avoidant" as if labeling the pattern alone explains everything. But true understanding of attachment is not found in labels. It's discovered through self-inquiry, through the slow and sometimes painful realization that much of what we call love is in fact a replay of very old, very familiar relational wounds.

Your attachment style is not a sentence—it's a story. And like any story, it can evolve. The first step in that evolution is understanding what story you're telling yourself in relationships, and where that story began.

Secure attachment is not perfection. It's not the absence of conflict or the presence of constant harmony. Rather, it's the ability to remain emotionally present and regulated when connection is threatened. It's the deep knowing, often implicit, that you are loved not because you're perfect, but because you are you. Those with secure attachment tend to be able to express their needs clearly, listen without becoming defensive, and allow space in relationships without panicking or withdrawing. They don't idealize others, nor do they devalue intimacy. Instead, they move with a sense of internal security that allows them to navigate closeness and autonomy with relative ease.

Securely attached individuals typically received consistent, attuned caregiving in early life. When they cried, someone came. When they explored, someone watched. When they were overwhelmed, someone helped them regulate. These early messages—"You are safe," "You matter," "I'm here and I'll be here again"—formed a nervous system that trusts relationships, even when challenged. That trust is not naive. It simply means the person doesn't expect abandonment around every corner or disconnection after every disagreement.

But for many, early relationships were less predictable. Maybe love was available but conditional. Maybe comfort was given sporadically, or not at all. Maybe closeness was threatening because it came paired with volatility, control, or intrusion. In such environments, children adapt. They learn to organize their emotional needs around the behaviors of those they depend on most. And this is how insecure attachment patterns take root.

Anxious attachment emerges when love feels unpredictable— there one moment and gone the next. The child in this environment becomes hyper-attuned to signs of closeness and distance. They learn to anticipate abandonment, to monitor for rejection, to cling in order to feel safe. As adults, those with anxious attachment often fear that their partner is going to leave, withdraw, or replace them. They may seek constant reassurance, become preoccupied with the relationship, or find it difficult to enjoy moments of solitude without imagining worst-case scenarios.

This isn't about being "too emotional" or "needy"—it's about early nervous systems trying to create stability where there was none. A person with an anxious pattern isn't flawed; they simply learned that closeness can't be trusted to stay unless they work to hold it tightly. Unfortunately, that very gripping often strains the connection they seek to protect, reinforcing their fear and deepening the cycle.

Avoidant attachment, on the other hand, develops in environments where vulnerability felt unsafe or unreciprocated. Perhaps emotions were met with disinterest or even punishment. Perhaps independence was rewarded, while emotional expression was shamed. Over time, the child learns to suppress their emotional needs in order to maintain connection, or at least maintain dignity. They become skilled at self-reliance—not because they don't need others, but because they've learned not to expect others to show up in ways that matter.

As adults, avoidantly attached individuals may appear aloof, self-sufficient, or uncomfortable with deep emotional intimacy. They may downplay the importance of relationships, delay commitment, or find reasons to create distance just as a relationship starts to feel real. But beneath the surface is often a longing for closeness that feels terrifying to admit. Vulnerability feels like a trap, not a bridge. So they protect themselves through emotional distance, intellectualization, or disengagement.

Both anxious and avoidant styles are strategies—elegant, intelligent adaptations to relational trauma. One strategy says, "If I stay close enough, maybe I won't be left." The other says, "If I stay far enough away, maybe I won't be hurt." And in some cases, people develop a blend of both, often called disorganized attachment. Here, the person longs for closeness but fears it at the same time. They may pursue a partner, then retreat the moment things become emotionally intense. They may sabotage connection even as they crave it. Disorganized patterns often stem from environments where caregivers were a source of both comfort and fear, where the child had no clear way to organize their attachment needs.

Understanding your style is not an invitation to self-diagnose and stop there. It's an opportunity to become curious, to observe yourself without judgment. Do you find yourself hyper-focused on your partner's mood, needing constant confirmation of their feelings for you? That may be an echo of anxious attachment. Do you tend to shut down when someone gets too close or demands emotional availability? That could point toward avoidant patterns. Do you feel like you want intimacy but never feel quite safe when you get it? You may be navigating disorganized territory.

This awareness, though uncomfortable at times, is the beginning of transformation. Because attachment is not fixed. Neuroscience now confirms what mystics and therapists have long intuited: the brain—and the heart—can change. Secure attachment can be earned. Through consistent self-regulation, compassionate introspection, healthy relationships, and often therapeutic support, individuals can rewire the relational patterns that once governed them unconsciously.

One of the most powerful ways this transformation begins is through self-parenting. If your early caregivers couldn't offer the security you needed, you can begin to offer it to yourself. This doesn't mean becoming self-sufficient to the point of isolation. It means creating a foundation of internal safety so that relationships become expressions of connection, not survival mechanisms. For the anxiously attached person, this might look like learning to self-soothe when anxiety arises, learning to trust their worth without needing another person to reflect it constantly. For the avoidantly attached, it might mean learning to stay present when emotions become uncomfortable, to share inner experiences even when it feels exposed.

Healthy relationships can be powerful healing spaces. Being in connection with someone who is securely attached can provide a new model for what love can be. But even this isn't a magic fix. The real work is internal. No partner can make you feel secure if you don't trust yourself to handle connection. No partner can give you safety if you are constantly abandoning yourself in fear.

What begins to shift, with time, is not just how you act but how you interpret others' actions. The anxiously attached person who once saw a delayed text as rejection learns to see it as neutrality. The avoidantly attached individual who once perceived emotional closeness as suffocating begins to recognize it as intimacy. The nervous system stops bracing for abandonment or intrusion, and starts settling into the unfamiliar but healing rhythm of trust.

Understanding your attachment style is not about fixing yourself—it's about meeting yourself. It's about honoring the ways your system has protected you, and gently guiding it toward connection that doesn't hurt. And as you do this, love stops being a battlefield or a puzzle. It becomes what it was always meant to be: a place of growth, reflection, and the exquisite unfolding of presence, moment by moment.

9.2 Earned Security Through Conscious Relationship

To believe that one's attachment style is fixed is to overlook one of the greatest truths of the human experience: that we are designed to grow, heal, and transform through connection. While our early relational experiences shape the architecture of our nervous system and beliefs about love, they do not define us indefinitely. Secure attachment is not something you either have or don't—it is something you can cultivate. It is not only inherited; it can be earned.

The term "earned secure attachment" refers to the process by which someone, often with a history of relational trauma or insecurity, becomes capable of developing secure, emotionally responsive, and stable patterns in adult relationships. This is not a concept rooted in wishful thinking—it is grounded in the science of neuroplasticity, which shows that the brain is constantly changing in response to experience. This is not to say the process is fast or easy. It requires presence, consistency, and above all, awareness. But it is possible.

Our brains adapt to survive the environments we grow up in. If closeness was unreliable, our minds learned to brace for abandonment. If vulnerability was punished, we learned to armor up. But when we begin to experience new forms of safety—when someone stays even after we reveal our shame, when a conflict doesn't lead to abandonment, when emotional availability becomes the norm instead of the exception—the brain begins to take notice. Slowly, it starts to loosen its grip on old defense mechanisms and forms new neural pathways that tell a different story: one of possibility, trust, and reciprocity.

What rewires the brain is not intensity, but consistency. A single beautiful date does not undo years of fear. A fleeting connection does not erase attachment wounds. But repeated experiences of attunement—being seen, heard, and responded to with warmth—begin to send a different message to the nervous system. The amygdala, the part of the brain responsible for detecting threats, becomes less reactive. The prefrontal cortex, responsible for regulation and reflection, becomes more engaged. Over time, the body starts to believe: maybe I don't have to panic when they don't text back. Maybe closeness doesn't mean I'll be consumed. Maybe love doesn't have to hurt.

One of the most powerful tools in this rewiring process is the act of repair. In secure relationships, conflict is not avoided—it is navigated. There is room for rupture, because there is a shared commitment to repair. When two people disagree, misunderstand, or even hurt each other, what matters most is not perfection, but what happens afterward. Do they come back? Do they acknowledge the pain? Do they make space for the emotions involved without defensiveness or blame?

Each time repair happens, a new message is written into the relational nervous system: "I can mess up and still be loved." "We can disagree and still come closer." "It's safe to tell the truth." These experiences are often more transformative than periods of peace. They show us that love is not fragile, that it can stretch, bend, and mend. And they train us to stay open even when our instinct is to flee or attack.

Of course, not all healing can or should be outsourced to another person. One of the most essential elements of earning secure attachment is the development of internal security. That means learning how to sit with your own discomfort without demanding someone else fix it. It means cultivating the capacity to regulate your emotions, to soothe your nervous system, to name your needs without collapsing into desperation or retreat. It means becoming the kind of person you would feel safe being close to.

This internal security begins with awareness. The ability to pause and ask: "What's really happening here?" instead of reacting impulsively. It continues with practices—breathwork, journaling, therapy, somatic movement—that help the body learn it is safe now, even if it wasn't before. It includes self-compassion, especially when you fall into old patterns. And over time, it begins to include a new sense of identity: not the wounded child longing for someone to fill the void, but the adult who knows they are worthy of love and capable of giving it in return.

To earn secure attachment is to rewrite your story—not by erasing the past, but by creating new chapters, full of presence, repair, and relational truth.

9.3 Creating Secure Relationships Regardless of History

Healing is deeply personal, but it is never solitary. The nervous system learns best in the presence of another. While internal work is essential, the container in which we relate—our choice of partner, the agreements we co-create, the rituals we honor—can either support or sabotage our growth. Building a secure relationship, especially after years of emotional turbulence or confusion, requires both courage and clarity.

The first step is often the hardest: learning to recognize who is capable of safe connection, and who is not. For those accustomed to insecurity, safety can feel boring. Chaos may masquerade as chemistry. The person who doesn't trigger your anxiety may not spark the same obsessive longing, but that's precisely the point. They don't feed the old pattern; they offer something new. Choosing a secure partner isn't about perfection. It's about emotional availability, communication, and the willingness to grow together.

Secure people are not without flaws. They may be slow to open up or make mistakes in communication. But they are grounded. They return. They don't manipulate through silence, or punish through withdrawal. They listen when you speak about your fears. They don't escalate when you express a need. Being with a secure partner doesn't mean you'll never feel triggered. But it does mean there is a foundation of stability—a relational floor you can land on when the winds of your past start blowing again.

But here's the deeper truth: even if you're not with a securely attached partner, you can still create secure dynamics. Secure functioning is not a personality trait; it's a relational practice. It is something two people choose, again and again, through their actions. That means you can become the secure base—not just for your partner, but for yourself. You can be the one who listens when emotions run high, who stays when things get hard, who communicates with honesty and kindness.

This doesn't mean becoming the caretaker or therapist in your relationship. It means modeling the behavior you want to receive. If you long for openness, be open. If you want emotional availability, practice sharing your truth. If you want safety, offer safety. Often, this kind of grounded presence inspires the same in others. Not always—but often. And when it doesn't, you gain clarity about whether the relationship can meet you where you are now, rather than where you were before.

Secure relationships don't just happen. They are created, moment by moment, through intentionality. One of the most powerful tools in this creation is the relationship container. Think of it like a structure—an agreement between two people that outlines how they want to show up for each other. This container can include rituals (like regular check-ins, shared practices, or digital boundaries), shared language (using certain words to signal emotional states), or commitments (like always repairing after a disagreement before going to bed angry).

These containers are not restrictive. They are expansive. They give the relationship form, so that the content—love, intimacy, growth—can flourish. Without them, we often revert to autopilot, which usually means replaying old stories. With them, we create a shared reality where both people feel seen, supported, and sovereign.

Boundaries are part of this container too. A secure relationship is not one where everything is shared, but one where everything that *needs* to be shared *can* be. It's not about fusion. It's about freedom in connection. Each person retains their individuality, their truth, their vision—and yet there is a shared space where those individualities meet and co-create something bigger than either one alone.

Security also means having the courage to say what's true, even when it's uncomfortable. It means bringing up the small ruptures before they grow into chasms. It means taking ownership of your reactions, and also holding your partner accountable when necessary. It means understanding that connection is not a constant—it is something we return to, over and over, by choice.

And perhaps most importantly, secure relationships allow for evolution. They make room for change. Who you are today is not who you will be in five years. A healthy connection adapts, listens, and grows alongside you. It doesn't demand you stay the same. It honors your process.

Regardless of your past, of how chaotic or lonely your early years were, you can learn to create relationships that feel like home. That reflect not your wounds, but your wholeness. You can choose people who see your heart, not just your survival strategies. And you can build dynamics rooted not in fear, but in reverence—for yourself, for your partner, and for the sacred dance between two human beings learning how to love each other well.

To be securely attached is not to never feel afraid, or to never question. It is to know, deep down, that you can face those fears. That you can question and still stay. That love is not the absence of rupture, but the presence of return. It is not static safety, but a living, breathing container of mutual care.

And that is something worth building, again and again, with tenderness and truth.

Chapter 10: The Ripple Effect — How Healthy Relationships Transform Communities

"Be the change you wish to see in the world." — Mahatma Gandhi

10.1 Modeling Conscious Relationship

There's a moment in every healing journey when the work begins to echo beyond the individual. After months or years of self-inquiry, boundary-setting, emotional regulation, and vulnerability, a subtle shift begins to unfold—not just internally, but externally. The way people respond to you changes. Conversations begin to carry more honesty. Conflicts deflate before they explode. The world, once a maze of emotional landmines, becomes a place of possibility. You've changed, yes. But so has everything you touch. This is the ripple effect of conscious relationship work: when your inner transformation quietly begins to transform those around you.

We often imagine healing as a solitary path—something we do in the privacy of a journal, in a therapy office, or in tearful, silent realizations. But emotional growth is relational by nature. The nervous system evolves in connection. The mind rewires in relationship. And so, as you begin to embody new ways of relating—new ways of speaking, listening, setting boundaries, and showing love—others notice. Sometimes consciously, sometimes not. But your way of being becomes a living example of what's possible. It becomes an invitation.

Humans are wired for resonance. Through mechanisms like mirror neurons, we automatically pick up on and reflect the emotional and behavioral states of others. This is why being around someone who is grounded and self-regulated can have an almost calming effect, even without words. It's why a single emotionally available person in a room can shift the tone of an entire group. Emotional health is not just contagious—it is magnetic. It draws out the parts in others that long to be safe, seen, and stable.

This resonance is not about perfection. In fact, one of the most powerful gifts you can offer your family, your partner, your coworkers, or your community is not flawless behavior, but transparent process. When you model what it looks like to feel a difficult emotion without acting it out, to apologize without collapsing, to express a need without blame, you are quietly teaching others what it means to be in conscious relationship. You're not just saying, "Here's how to love better." You're showing it. You're embodying it.

Nowhere is this ripple more profound than within families. When one person in a family system begins to heal, they inevitably come into contact with generational patterns—ways of relating that have been passed down not through malice, but through habit and survival. Maybe your parents didn't know how to talk about feelings because no one ever talked to them about theirs. Maybe emotional expression was discouraged, or love was confused with control. These patterns, though inherited, are not inescapable.

When you decide to sit with your discomfort instead of projecting it, when you choose to respond instead of react, when you refuse to repeat what was done to you—consciously or unconsciously—you begin to interrupt those cycles. You start to write a different story, one that says pain can end with you. This doesn't mean you cut off everyone who hasn't done the same work. It means you relate differently. You hold boundaries without aggression. You offer compassion without enabling. You stay rooted in your values, even when others are thrown off by the change.

And if you have children—biological, adopted, chosen, or metaphorical—the ripple becomes even more visible. Children don't learn emotional intelligence from lectures or lessons. They learn it from experience. From watching how the adults around them handle stress. From seeing how repair happens after conflict. From feeling what it's like to be heard, even when they don't have the words to explain themselves.

When you raise a child in an environment of secure attachment—where their emotions are mirrored rather than minimized, where their needs are taken seriously without being indulged, where love is consistent rather than contingent—you are not just helping them feel safe in the moment. You are helping them build a blueprint for every relationship they will ever have. That blueprint will shape how they love, how they parent, how they lead, and how they see themselves.

This is the quiet revolution. It happens in kitchens, at dinner tables, during bedtime routines. It happens when a child learns that their tears are not a problem to be fixed, but a truth to be held. It happens when a teenager feels safe enough to share their fear because they trust you won't make it about you. It happens when your presence communicates, without needing to be said, "You matter. You're safe. I'm here."

But the impact of conscious relational practice doesn't end at home. It follows you into every domain of life—especially the professional one. We like to think of work and emotion as separate. We enter offices with polished faces and leave our inner worlds at the door. But the truth is, our relationship patterns follow us to work. The same dynamics that play out in our personal lives—avoidance, people-pleasing, reactivity, defensiveness—show up in meetings, in emails, in leadership styles.

When someone brings emotional intelligence into a professional environment, it changes everything. Suddenly, communication becomes clearer, not just more polite. Feedback becomes collaborative rather than critical. Leadership shifts from control to inspiration. Conflict, instead of being avoided or escalated, becomes a space for innovation and growth.

This doesn't mean you become the therapist of your team. It means you model what it looks like to stay regulated under pressure. To admit when you're wrong without losing authority. To set limits without becoming rigid. To humanize the workplace without sacrificing professionalism.

Organizations that embrace relational awareness tend to be more resilient. Teams communicate more effectively. Burnout decreases. Creativity increases. People feel safer to share ideas, voice concerns, and take healthy risks. And it often starts with one person—someone willing to lead not with force, but with presence.

Conscious relationship work is not selfish. It is one of the most generous acts you can offer your community. Because when you do the inner work to regulate your nervous system, clarify your boundaries, and own your projections, you become a safer person to be around. You create space for others to show up as they are, not as who they think they have to be. You contribute to an atmosphere where vulnerability is not punished, where truth is not weaponized, where connection is not conditional.

And this kind of presence reverberates. It doesn't require a platform or a title. It shows up in the way you treat a stranger, the way you respond to irritation, the way you stay open in a moment of tension. Every small act of consciousness sends ripples outward—toward your friends, your colleagues, your family, your children, and yes, even toward the strangers who catch a glimpse of your quiet integrity.

We often underestimate the power of our relational influence. We assume we need to be experts or teachers to make a difference. But the truth is, your most powerful impact comes not from what you say, but from how you live. The way you love, the way you listen, the way you recover from mistakes—these become the curriculum. These are the lessons people remember.

So if you've ever questioned whether the deep, often invisible work of emotional growth matters, let this be your reminder: it does. Not just for you, but for everyone who crosses your path. The way you relate is your legacy. And when you choose to relate with consciousness, you help build a world where love is not just a longing, but a lived reality. One breath, one boundary, one moment at a time.

10.2 Creating Circles of Support

Growth, when it's real, eventually demands a new ecosystem. As you begin to shift internally—healing your wounds, regulating your nervous system, setting clearer boundaries—the world around you will respond. Some relationships will flourish with your evolution, meeting you in the newfound spaciousness of your presence. Others will begin to crack under the pressure of your refusal to play old roles. What once felt familiar may now feel draining. What used to pass as connection may now seem like energetic entanglement. And in this space of transition, one of the most essential yet often overlooked needs becomes clear: community.

Healing cannot live in isolation. Nor can it survive in environments that constantly pull you back into outdated patterns. There comes a point when growth is no longer just about what happens in your journal, therapy room, or meditation cushion. It becomes about who you spend your time with. Who you allow to see your rawness. Who you trust with your truths. Who reminds you of who you're becoming, especially when you forget.

Choosing your inner circle is not an act of judgment—it is an act of stewardship. You are curating the emotional landscape in which your future self will unfold. If that circle is filled with people who belittle your boundaries, mock your vulnerability, or subtly encourage your regression, your nervous system will remain on high alert. You will feel unsafe being real. You'll shrink yourself to stay connected, mistaking survival for belonging.

But when you build a circle composed of those who see your light and not just your wounds—who hold space for your process without making it about them—you begin to thrive. These are the people who challenge you to grow without shaming you for

117

where you are. They don't flinch when you're messy. They celebrate your breakthroughs but don't demand your perfection. They listen without fixing. They speak truth without cruelty. In their presence, you remember that connection doesn't have to cost you your integrity.

This kind of community doesn't happen by accident. It requires discernment, vulnerability, and, sometimes, grief. You may have to outgrow relationships you thought would last forever. You may need to lovingly distance yourself from family members who constantly trigger your dysregulation. You might find yourself sitting in the discomfort of loneliness before your new community forms. But this in-between space is not a punishment—it's a rite of passage.

In healthy support circles, a beautiful dynamic begins to emerge: mutual mentorship. No one is the guru. No one is above or below. Instead, each person brings their own medicine to the fire. At times, you are the one offering wisdom. At others, you are the one receiving it. You become mirrors for each other—not to judge, but to reflect what's possible. The hierarchy of traditional help collapses, and something more egalitarian, more alive, takes its place.

These relationships are rooted in trust and reciprocity. They are not transactional. They don't keep score. You can go months without talking and still return to the same depth. You can share your shadows without fear of gossip. You can ask for support without shame. And most importantly, you can say no, set a limit, or ask for space without jeopardizing the connection.

At the core of all of this lies the sacred art of witnessing. To witness someone means to be fully present without trying to control, fix, or manage their process. It means sitting in the fire with them—not to extinguish it, but to remind them they are not alone. Sacred witnessing is powerful because it honors agency. It doesn't treat others as projects. It doesn't impose timelines or advice. It simply says, "I see you. I trust you. I'm here."

Holding space in this way requires maturity. Without it, witnessing can slip into codependency. You might find yourself over-functioning, rescuing, or emotionally merging with someone else's pain. This does not help them heal—it only relieves your own discomfort with their discomfort. True witnessing involves boundaries. You know where you end and they begin. You remain grounded in your own body while being present with theirs. You recognize that their healing is theirs to do, and your presence is a gift—not a solution.

When enough people begin to live this way—choosing their inner circles with care, engaging in mutual mentorship, and practicing sacred witnessing—a new kind of community begins to take shape. One that isn't based on performance or pretense, but on authenticity and connection. One that doesn't demand conformity but celebrates diversity of expression. One that doesn't just support individual healing, but amplifies it.

This is what it means to create a circle of support: a living, breathing organism made of people who choose growth, again and again, together.

10.3 Service Through Relationship

If you've walked this path long enough, something inevitable begins to happen. Your healing stops being just about you. Yes, it started with your wounds—your heartbreaks, your childhood, your pain. It required turning inward, facing demons, grieving old losses, and building new habits. But eventually, healing deepens into something quieter, wider, and more rooted in service. You begin to realize that your relational integrity, your ability to love and be loved well, is not only a personal victory. It is a contribution. A form of activism. A prayer embodied.

We tend to imagine activism as protest, legislation, or public demonstration. But relationship, when practiced consciously, is one of the most powerful forms of cultural transformation available to us. Every time you choose to respond instead of react, you model a new possibility. Every time you refuse to pass on your pain, you interrupt a cycle. Every time you love without controlling, listen without judgment, or forgive without enabling, you are healing not only yourself but the field around you.

This is what it means for love to become service. It's not about martyrdom or self-sacrifice. It's about letting the way you relate be your offering to a hurting world. When you raise your children with empathy instead of shame, when you end a relationship with respect instead of vengeance, when you create a home where boundaries are honored and emotions are welcomed—you are planting seeds. Those seeds don't just bear fruit in your own life. They influence how others feel, think, relate, and evolve.

For the next generation, this is everything. Children and teenagers learn more from what we model than what we say. You can talk to a young person about emotional intelligence, but if they see you avoid conflict, lash out under pressure, or shrink in the face of your own truth, that is what they will internalize. On the other hand, if you show them what it looks like to apologize, to regulate yourself, to stand up for your needs without aggression—they carry that blueprint with them.

Mentorship doesn't always look like formal teaching. Often, it's simply being the adult who listens. The one who doesn't dismiss their feelings. The one who reflects their worth back to them, especially when they can't see it. The one who doesn't pretend to have it all together but shows them what it looks like to keep learning, keep trying, and keep showing up.

Through these acts, the transmission of dysfunction begins to slow. It doesn't disappear overnight, but it weakens. It stutters. And in its place, a new legacy begins to take root—not one of pain management, but of emotional fluency. Of relational resilience. Of love that doesn't consume but liberates.

And it's not just children who benefit. Communities as a whole begin to transform when relationships shift. Many of society's most persistent wounds—addiction, violence, loneliness, systemic inequality—are rooted in unmet relational needs. When people don't feel safe, connected, or seen, they turn to whatever gives them relief. That might be substances. That might be control. That might be dissociation. But at the root, it's all about love. Or more precisely, the absence of it.

If we want to address the mental health crisis, we must look beyond individual pathology and into relational ecosystems. If we want to reduce violence, we must ask how emotional regulation and attachment security are being taught—or neglected—in homes, schools, and workplaces. If we want to create more compassionate societies, we must begin by creating more compassionate relationships.

This is not abstract. It's not idealistic. It's intensely practical. A regulated nervous system in one person can help calm a chaotic environment. A securely attached couple can model what love looks like for an entire neighborhood. A workplace that values communication and mutual respect can ripple into families, friendships, and futures. The changes may not make headlines, but they make homes. They make schools safer. They make communities more resilient.

This is the essence of service through relationship. Not in grand gestures, but in daily choices. You don't need to save the world. You just need to love well. To keep showing up. To keep growing. To keep choosing connection over control, presence over performance, and truth over comfort.

Because the truth is, relationships are not just where we get hurt. They're also where we heal. They are the vessels through which culture is transmitted, values are taught, and change is made real. And when you commit to relating from a place of consciousness, integrity, and care, you are not just building a better life. You are helping build a better world.

Conclusion: The Ongoing Journey – Relationship as Spiritual Practice

"Love is not something we give or get; it is something that we are." – Wayne Dyer

There is no final chapter in the work of love. No finish line, no moment where one arrives fully healed, immune to triggers, impervious to fear or judgment. Relationship, like life itself, is an unfolding process—a spiral rather than a straight line. Each loop revisits old lessons in deeper ways, offering new layers of insight, compassion, and challenge. And if we're paying attention, if we remain willing to meet life with open eyes and a steady heart, every relationship becomes both teacher and temple, revealing the sacred within the ordinary.

This book has walked you through the intricate dance of relational transformation: from the excavation of your emotional blueprint to the healing of trauma, from the integration of inner polarities to the cultivation of secure attachment, from the reshaping of communication to the alchemy of conflict. But none of this was meant to be consumed as information alone. The ideas, reflections, and practices offered were not here to be mastered and then shelved—they were invitations. Invitations to turn your life itself into the curriculum. To walk each day as a practitioner, not of perfection, but of presence. To view your interactions not as distractions from your spiritual path, but as the path itself.

And what makes that path so powerful—so quietly revolutionary—is its ordinariness. It's not just found in the grand moments of romance or reconciliation. It's in the micro-choices: pausing before a reaction, softening into vulnerability, owning your part without shame. It's in the way you speak to your child after a long day, or how you respond to your partner's fear. It's in your willingness to ask for what you need, and your capacity to receive the no without collapse. These moments, so easy to overlook, are the real altars of relational practice.

Yet this path is not easy. To commit to conscious relationship is to walk with your eyes open, knowing full well that love will stretch you, reveal you, and sometimes undo you. It is to choose growth over comfort, honesty over harmony, and intimacy over illusion. It means you will fail—often. You will say the wrong thing. You will revert to old habits. You will misread signals, miscommunicate, misunderstand. But the work is not in getting it right—it's in how you return. How you repair. How you forgive yourself and try again.

This is where the journey becomes spiritual. Because when you begin to see every rupture as an opportunity for reconnection, every irritation as a mirror, every trigger as a trailhead to healing, you stop seeing your relationships as problems to fix or people to manage. Instead, they become your path back to yourself. They become the very terrain where your soul stretches into form, where your ego softens and your essence rises.

This reframing—this spiritual lens—is what allows the work to continue beyond the pages of this book. Because no technique, no framework, no perfect script can protect you from the complexity of being human with other humans. What carries you forward is not a system but a devotion. A devotion to love as a way of being, not a feeling. A devotion to truth, even when it's uncomfortable. A devotion to presence, even when your nervous system wants to run. And perhaps most importantly, a devotion to seeing yourself and others not as projects to be perfected, but as sacred beings already worthy of care and connection.

To stay on this path requires nourishment. Just as your physical body needs rest and food, your relational capacity needs replenishment. That means returning to the practices that anchor you—meditation, journaling, somatic awareness, therapy, nature. It means checking in with yourself regularly: What am I feeling? What am I needing? Where am I abandoning myself to please or protect? And it means continuing to surround yourself with people who call forth your highest self, not through flattery, but through honesty, reflection, and love.

The truth is, you cannot walk this path alone. Nor should you. While the inner work is yours to do, the outer support makes it sustainable. Seek out spaces that foster authentic connection: support groups, spiritual communities, relational workshops, or simply circles of trusted friends where depth is welcome and masks are optional. In those spaces, you are reminded that you are not the only one stumbling forward with a heart that wants to love but doesn't always know how. You are not the only one unraveling generational knots, soothing inner children, and learning to speak in the language of truth. There is comfort in shared struggle. There is power in communal growth.

And as you grow, your relationships will evolve. Some will fall away, not with bitterness, but with gratitude for the role they played. Others will deepen, not because they become easier, but because they become more honest. New ones will emerge— unexpected, expansive, aligned with who you are becoming. But through it all, one relationship remains constant: the one with yourself. Every boundary you set, every need you express, every time you pause instead of explode, you are reinforcing the sacred bond between your inner and outer worlds.

Let that be your compass. Let your relationship with yourself be the template for how you relate to others. When you are kind to your inner voice, kindness flows outward. When you forgive your own humanity, you make room for others' imperfection.

When you cultivate joy, presence, and truth within, your relationships stop being sources of drama and become sources of vitality. And slowly, without trying to change the world, you begin to do just that.

Because when enough people commit to this work—not as an intellectual pursuit but as a way of living—something shifts. Families begin to heal. Communities begin to soften. The cycles of violence, avoidance, and disconnection lose their grip. And in their place, something ancient and new takes root: love that liberates rather than binds. Love that holds rather than controls. Love that tells the truth, even when it shakes.

This is the path forward. Not toward a perfect relationship, but toward a conscious one. Not toward a painless life, but toward a meaningful one. Not toward a sanitized version of connection, but toward a raw, radiant, real one—where you bring all of yourself and invite others to do the same.

As you close this book, know that the real work begins now. Not in the concepts, but in the moments. In how you greet your partner after a hard day. In how you hold yourself when shame creeps in. In how you stay, speak, or walk away. In how you love—not as a performance, but as a practice.

So take this journey into your life. Let it shape your mornings, your meetings, your phone calls, your family dinners. Let it infuse your relationships with presence, courage, and grace. Let it remind you, again and again, that every interaction is a doorway. And behind each doorway is an invitation—to grow, to soften, to listen, to love.

You are not walking alone. Across time, culture, and geography, others are walking too. Some ahead, some behind, some right beside you. Together, we are reshaping the world, one relationship at a time.

And it begins—always—with you.

www.ingramcontent.com/pod-product-compliance
Lightning Source LLC
Chambersburg PA
CBHW071135280326
41935CB00010B/1240